Textbook for course **"Fun With Designing"**

First Edition – December 2024

ISBN: 978-93-5780-661-9

AF675212

Author : Vinay Bhatt.

Learnincreation.com

Price : 550 Rs. (INR)

Cover, Layout & Illustration – Learnincreation

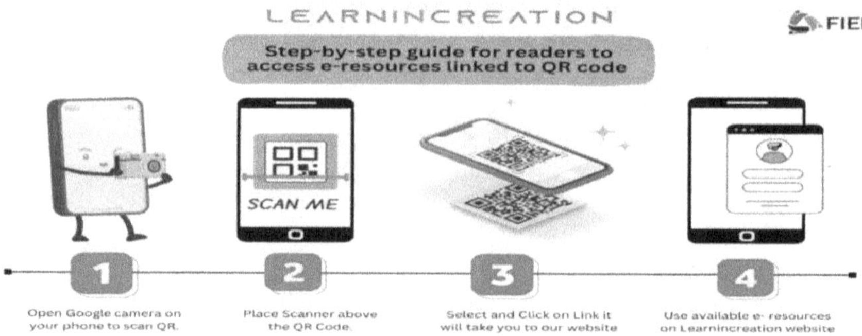

SCAN ME

For WEBSITE **To FIND STUDY CENTRE** **WATCH**
us on YOUTUBE

What's Waiting for You in This Book?

Are you ready to embark on an exciting adventure into the world of web design? Well, buckle up because we're about to dive in! Here's a sneak peek of what you'll be learning in this book. We've broken it down into easy-to-follow chapters, so you can build your skills step by step, and most importantly—have fun along the way!

1. **HTML Fundamentals: The Building Blocks of the Web**
    - Imagine you're constructing a house. HTML is your foundation—without it, there's nothing to build on! In this section, you'll learn how to structure and organize content on a website. You'll get hands-on with the essential tags and elements that make up a webpage. Get ready to create your first web page!
2. **CSS Styling: Turn Plain to Pretty**
    - Now that you've built the skeleton of your website, let's make it shine! CSS is your toolbox for making a website visually stunning. In this chapter, you'll add colors, fonts, and layouts to your pages. It's like choosing the perfect paint colors and furniture for your house—only this time, it's all on your screen!
3. **JavaScript Interactivity: Making Your Website Come Alive**
    - Ready to bring your website to life? This is where the magic happens! JavaScript allows you to add interactive elements, like buttons, forms, and dynamic content. By the end of this section, you'll be able to create web pages that respond to user actions and look even more polished and functional.
4. **Project-Based Learning: From Theory to Reality**
    - Why just read when you can create? Throughout the book, you'll work on real-world projects that let you practice everything you've learned. No boring theory here—each project is designed to give you the experience you need to apply your skills right away and build something truly exciting!
5. **Best Practices: Secrets of Professional Designers**
    - Ever wonder how top designers make their websites look so effortless? In this section, you'll unlock insider tips and tricks that professionals use. You'll learn how to design websites that are not only beautiful but also user-friendly and accessible. These best practices will elevate your designs to the next level!

Each chapter is packed with practical examples, clear explanations, and hands-on exercises. The goal? To help you *not just* understand the concepts but also to feel confident applying them as you go. You won't just be a learner—you'll be a creator. By the end of this book, you'll have built your own stunning websites that you can be proud of.

So, are you ready to get started? Let's dive in and have some fun with design!

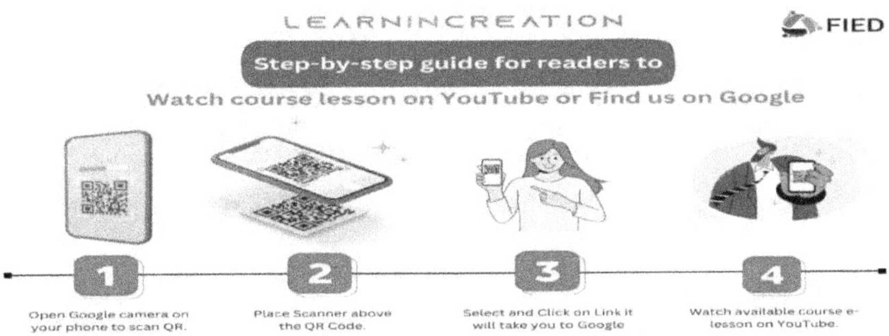
LEARNINCREATION
FIED
Step-by-step guide for readers to
Watch course lesson on YouTube or Find us on Google
1
Open Google camera on your phone to scan QR.
2
Place Scanner above the QR Code.
3
Select and Click on Link it will take you to Google
4
Watch available course e-lesson on YouTube.

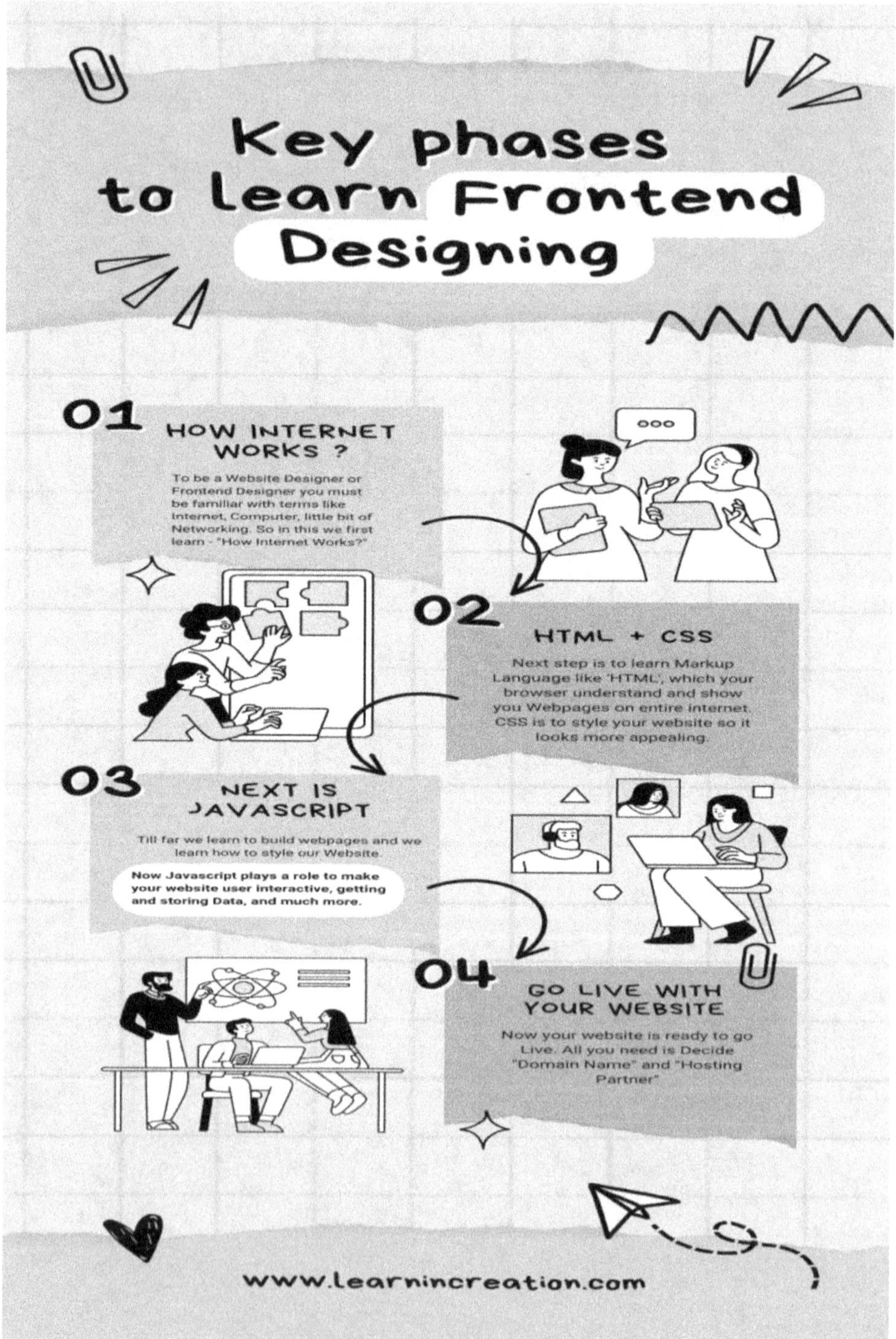
Key phases to learn Frontend Designing
01
HOW INTERNET WORKS ?
To be a Website Designer or Frontend Designer you must be familiar with terms like Internet, Computer, little bit of Networking. So in this we first learn - "How Internet Works?"
02
HTML + CSS
Next step is to learn Markup Language like 'HTML', which your browser understand and show you Webpages on entire internet. CSS is to style your website so it looks more appealing.
03
NEXT IS JAVASCRIPT
Till far we learn to build webpages and we learn how to style our Website.
Now Javascript plays a role to make your website user interactive, getting and storing Data, and much more.
04
GO LIVE WITH YOUR WEBSITE
Now your website is ready to go Live. All you need is Decide "Domain Name" and "Hosting Partner"
www.learnincreation.com

Introduction about Author

Hi there! I'm Vinay Bhatt, a full-stack web developer, Google-certified digital marketing expert, and ethical hacking enthusiast, based in Rudrapur, Uttarakhand, India. My journey into the world of technology started back in 2014 when I was working on my bachelor's degree in science (BSc.). Since then, I've spent years diving deep into web development, digital marketing, and cybersecurity, constantly learning and growing in this exciting field.

This book, *Fun with Designing*, is all about sharing what I've learned with you. Together, we'll explore the core concepts of HTML, CSS, and JavaScript—three essential skills for designing interactive and visually appealing websites. What I really love about web design is how hands-on it is, and that's exactly how I want you to approach this book. You'll find practical examples and exercises throughout, so you can immediately apply what you're learning and start building.

In addition to my work as a developer, I've also created **Learnincreation**, a platform dedicated to making computer science more accessible to everyone. I'm proud to share that it was incubated at **FIED (Foundation for Innovation and Entrepreneurship Development)** at IIM Kashipur in October 2023. I've also written books like **"Computer Fundamentals"**, all with the goal of making tech knowledge simpler and more approachable.

Join Me on This Journey

Whether you're a beginner or just looking to brush up on your skills, I'm confident that this book will guide you through the world of web design, step-by-step. So, grab your laptop, let's dive into HTML, CSS, and JavaScript, and start creating something amazing website together!

Course Objective

Welcome to *Fun with Design*! The primary goal of this e-book is to guide you through the exciting world of website designing using **HTML**, **CSS**, and **JavaScript**. Whether you're a student, a professional, or simply someone eager to dive into the world of web design, this course is for you.

In this e-book, you'll learn the fundamental concepts and techniques for creating stunning, functional websites. From building the structure of a webpage with HTML, to styling it with CSS, and adding interactivity using JavaScript, we'll cover it all. By the end of this course, you'll not only understand how to design websites but also how to bring them to life with engaging layouts and dynamic features.

Whether you're starting from scratch or looking to enhance your skills, this course is designed to be both informative and practical, giving you the tools you need to create websites that are both beautiful and user-friendly.

PREFACE

Welcome to the first edition of *Fun with Design*! This book is your introduction to the world of website design, offering a solid foundation in HTML, CSS, and JavaScript. Whether you're looking to start a career in web development or simply want to learn how to create your own websites with ease, this book is designed to guide you every step of the way.

In today's fast-paced digital world, where technologies are constantly evolving, we've made it our mission to provide clear, up-to-date explanations of all the essential topics related to web design. Our goal is to give you the tools and confidence to build stunning, functional websites, no matter your skill level.

We've worked hard to make this e-book as comprehensive and user-friendly as possible, and it's incredibly rewarding to see that many readers have embraced this approach. To all our readers, thank you for your trust and support. Your belief in this book motivates us to continue sharing knowledge and helping others grow in the field of web design.

Copyright & Disclaimer -

We continuously build new courses and update content of our website, tutorials or e-books time to time in order to build better interactive learning resources for student; however the content may contain typing error or inaccuracies, as there is always much more to learn and update, but if you discover any kind of inaccuracies or error in our website, e-books or in any content, please notify us at our mail address. It would be great help.

Write to Author

BEFORE YOU START

This beginner-friendly course will teach you everything you need to know about website development, starting from the very basics. If you've never written code or worked on web design before, this course will guide you through each step in an easy-to-understand way. You'll start by learning the core concepts of website design, such as layout, structure, and user experience. As you progress, you'll dive into HTML, CSS, and JavaScript, the three key technologies that power modern websites.

By the end of the course, you'll have a solid understanding of how websites are created and how these languages work together to build a fully functional website. This course is designed not only for students but also for anyone who is passionate about learning new skills, such as career changers, entrepreneurs, or people looking to enhance their knowledge in the digital world.

About the Book: This course is structured like a practical guide, designed to walk you through real-life examples and projects so you can practice and apply what you learn right away. It's packed with helpful tips, clear explanations, and step-by-step instructions, making it perfect for beginners who want to develop strong foundational skills in web development.

Career Opportunities: After completing this course, you'll be equipped with the skills to pursue a career in web development, an in-demand field with opportunities in various industries.

Whether you're interested in becoming a web designer, front-end developer, or even starting your own freelance business, the skills you gain from this course will open doors to numerous career paths in the growing tech industry. Web development is one of the most sought-after skills, and it's never been a better time to dive in!

Certification: To add more value to your learning journey, you have the option to receive a certificate upon completion of this course. This certificate, issued by **Learnincreation**, will showcase your newly acquired skills in web development and can enhance your resume. Additionally, if you prefer a more hands-on experience, you can join our in-person classes at our **Study Centre**, where you'll get direct guidance from our expert instructors.

Take the Next Step in Your Career: Whether you choose the online learning option or decide to join us at our Study Centre, this course will help you build a strong foundation for a successful career in web development.

Enroll today and get started on your journey to becoming a skilled web developer! Don't miss out on the opportunity to learn, grow, and earn your certificate.

TABLE OF CONTENTS

Chapter 1: Introduction to Web Design

1.1 How the Web Works?

The internet is an essential part of daily life, but understanding how it works is fundamental to building a website. At its core, the web operates through a **client-server model**.

- **Client**: This is the user's device (browser or app) that requests information from the server. Common browsers include Chrome, Firefox, and Safari.
- **Server**: A computer where all the website's data, files, and resources are stored.
- **Request/Response**: When you type in a website address, your browser (client) sends an **HTTP request** to the server. The server then sends back a response, which your browser interprets and displays as a webpage.

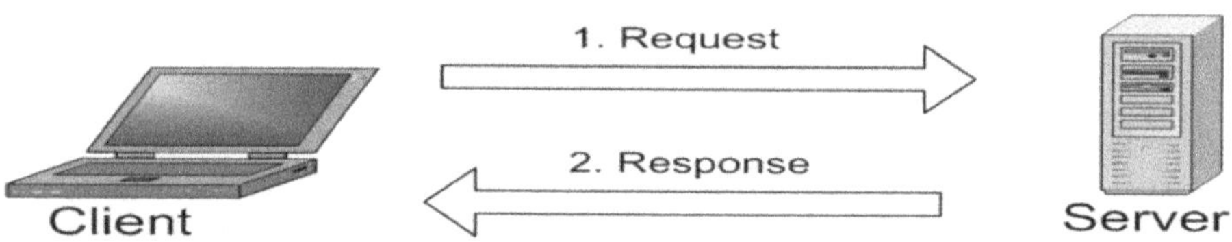

Key Technologies:

- **HTML**: HyperText Markup Language, used to create the structure and content.
- **CSS**: Cascading Style Sheets, used for styling and layout.
- **JavaScript**: Adds interactivity and functionality.

Example:
Imagine typing www.example.com in your browser. Your browser

makes an HTTP request to the server, and the server responds with an HTML file. Your browser then renders the HTML, applies styles from CSS, and runs JavaScript for any dynamic actions (like form submissions).

1.2 How Websites Help and Their Importance

Websites are indispensable in today's digital era, whether for communication, business, education, or entertainment. They provide:

- **Business Benefits**: Websites help companies promote their brand, sell products, and provide services. E-commerce websites like Amazon or eBay have revolutionized shopping by allowing global reach.
- **Educational Value**: Websites like Khan Academy or Coursera provide online learning, making education accessible to everyone, anywhere.
- **Communication**: Social media platforms (Facebook, Twitter) help individuals stay connected and interact with others.
- **Content Creation**: Platforms like YouTube or Medium allow users to create and share content, whether it's a video or a blog post.

Example:

- **Corporate Site**: Features sections like "About Us," "Services," "Contact" for customer engagement.
- **E-Commerce**: A product page with images, descriptions, prices, and a shopping cart feature.
- **Blog**: Regular posts about a particular topic, with the ability to comment and share.

1.3 Who Builds Websites and Why?

There are separate roles in website creation, each contributing to various aspects of a website.

- **Web Designer**: Focuses on the **visual elements** of a website, such as layout, fonts, colors, and overall appearance. They aim to create an aesthetically pleasing and user-friendly interface.
- **Web Developer**: A developer's job is to **code** and make the design functional. They use languages like HTML, CSS, and JavaScript.
- **Front-End Developer**: Works on the **user-facing part of the website** (what visitors see and interact with). They code using HTML, CSS, and JavaScript.
- **Back-End Developer**: Works on the **server-side**, handling things like databases, servers, and application logic.

1.4 What You Need to Learn to Build a Website.

To create a fully functional website, you need to master three primary technologies:

1. **HTML (HyperText Markup Language)**: This is the foundation of any webpage. It's used to define the structure of a webpage, such as headings, paragraphs, lists, links, images, etc.
2. **CSS (Cascading Style Sheets)**: CSS defines the presentation of the HTML structure. You can control fonts, colors, spacing, and layout with CSS.
3. **JavaScript**: This is used to add **dynamic behavior** to your site, like form validation, animations, and interactive features.

Example:

- **HTML**: A webpage has content in a structured form.
- **CSS**: That content is styled with colors, fonts, and layouts.
- **JavaScript**: Makes the website interactive, such as validating forms or displaying images on hover.

Chapter 2: Understanding

HTML

2.1 Introduction and History of HTML

HTML was created by **Tim Berners-Lee** in 1991 to enable researchers to share documents over the internet. HTML defines the structure of a webpage and is still the most widely used language on the web.

HTML is constantly evolving to meet new web needs. **HTML5** is the latest version and is widely used today, offering improved features like multimedia support (audio, video), semantic tags, and improved accessibility.

HTML Structure:

HTML documents follow a basic structure:

In HTML documents we use " **<!-- -->**" this syntax for writing comments related to work we do or function , design we make so we can later read comment to understand the code and its behaviours, also it will helps other developer to read and work on your code or understand them. So write anything in between this syntax " **<!-- hello i am a comment -->**" and browser will no longer read and execute them.

```
<!DOCTYPE html> <!-- define document type version of html file/ webpage -->
<html>  <!--html document start from here -->
  <head>  <!-- define head of html file, information in this section is related to web browser -->
    <meta charset="UTF-8">  <!-- define character set of html file -->
    <title>My First Webpage</title>  <!--define Title of your Webpage -->
  </head>  <!-- closing tag of head element -->
  <body>  <!-- opening tag of body element, work we do here will display on webpage body -->
    <h1>Welcome to My Website</h1>  <!-- Main Heading of our Webpage -->
    <p>This is a simple webpage built using HTML.</p>  <!-- to write paragraph in your webpage -->
  </body>  <!-- define our work end here, closing tag of body -->
</html>  <!-- closing tag of html file. -->
```

Explanation:

- <!DOCTYPE html>: Declares the document type and

HTML version.

- <html>: The root element that wraps the entire document.
- <head>: Contains meta-information like the page's title, character set, and linked resources (CSS, JavaScript).
- <body>: Contains the visible content (headings, paragraphs, images).

2.2 Setting Up Notepad++ on Your System

Notepad++ is a free code editor for writing HTML, CSS, and JavaScript. It's lightweight and simple to use. Here's how to set it up:

1. **Download** Notepad++ from https://notepad-plus-plus.org/.
2. **Install** by following the on-screen instructions.
3. **Create New File**: Open Notepad++ and create a new file with the .html extension to start writing HTML.

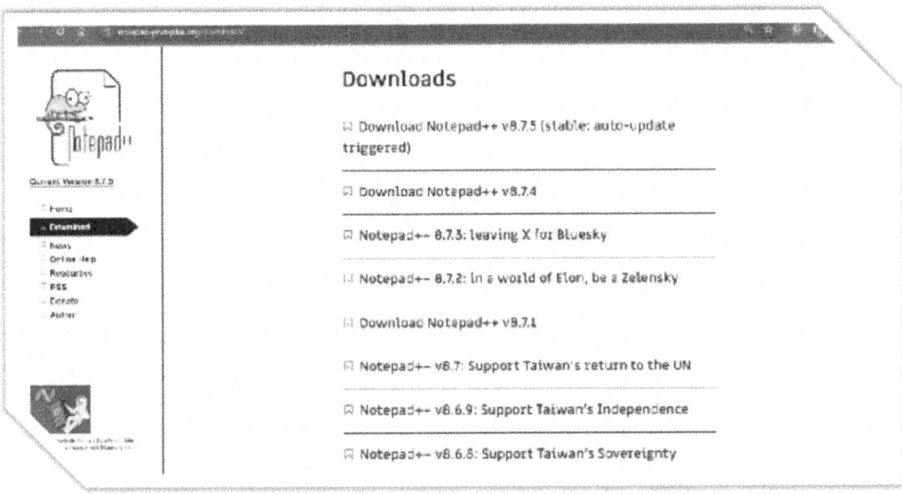

2.3 Components of a Website

A website is made up of several components, each playing a critical role in its development.

- **HTML**: Structures the webpage with headings, paragraphs, links, and more.
- **CSS**: Adds style, controlling fonts, colors, and layouts.
- **JavaScript**: Introduces interactivity, enabling features like animations, form validation, and dynamic content loading.
- **Images/Media**: Files such as images, videos, and audio that enrich the user experience.
- **Databases**: Store dynamic data such as user information, product listings, or blog posts.

Example:
A simple website could consist of:

- **HTML** for the structure (text, links).
- **CSS** for the style (colors, fonts).
- **JavaScript** for functionality (form validation, dynamic content).

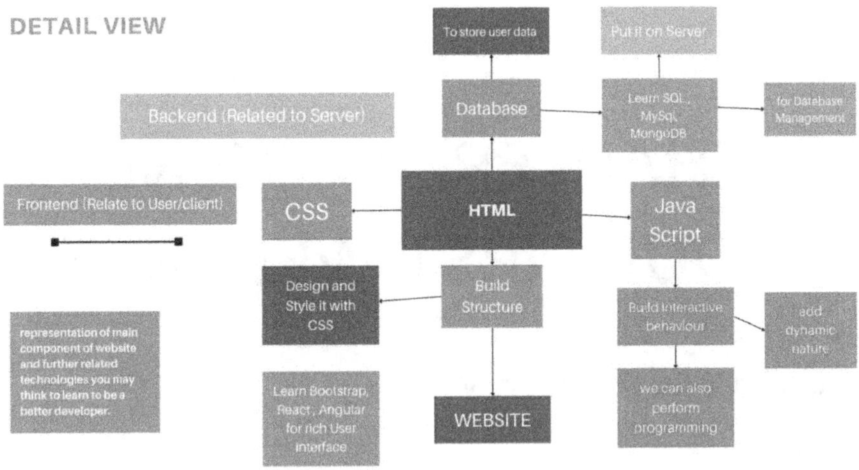
DETAIL VIEW
To store user data
Put it on Server
Backend (Related to Server)
Database
Learn SQL, MySql, MongoDB
for Database Management
Frontend (Relate to User/client)
CSS
HTML
Java Script
Design and Style it with CSS
Build Structure
Build Interactive behaviour
add dynamic nature
representation of main component of website and further related technologies you may think to learn to be a better developer.
Learn Bootstrap, React, Angular for rich User interface
WEBSITE
we can also perform programming

CHAPTER 3: CODING YOUR FIRST WEBPAGE

3.1 Let's Code Our First Webpage

Creating your first webpage can be a fun experience. Here's the simplest webpage you can create:

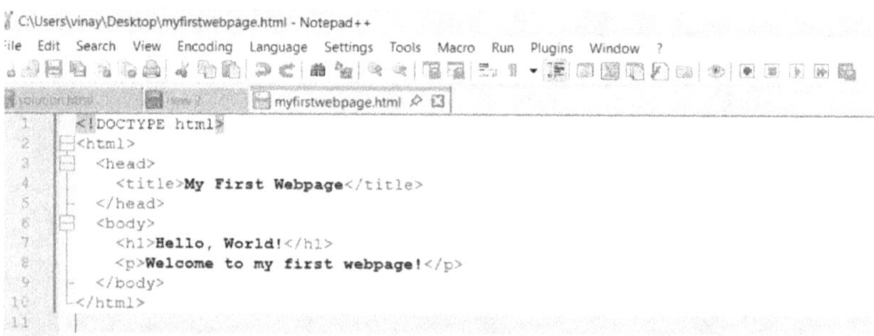

Explanation:

- <h1>: The most important heading.
- <p>: Defines a paragraph of text.

To view this webpage:

1. Copy the code and paste it into a Notepad++ file.
2. Save the file with a .html extension (e.g., index.html).

3. Open the file in any web browser to view your webpage.

> Don't forget to make your own file and run it, coding is all about practice and being hands on, don't forget to build your own handwritten notes also, it will helps you later in future.

3.2 HTML TAGS: THE BUILDING BLOCKS

HTML tags define the content structure. Some essential tags include:

- <h1> to <h6>: Headings, where <h1> is the largest, and <h6> is the smallest.
- <p>: for writing Paragraphs in your webpage.
- <a>: to add Links in your html webpage (to connect/ navigate it to another file).
- <img>: to add Images in your webpage, use alt=" " attribute for alternate name.

Example:

<a href="https://www.learnincreation.com">Click Here</a>

This creates a clickable link to "learnincreation.com", and Click Here will be display on body.

3.3 ELEMENTS, ATTRIBUTES, AND PARAMETERS : KEY CONCEPT

HTML is composed of **elements** defined by tags. These elements can have **attributes** that provide additional information.

- **Elements**: Represented by HTML tags like <h1>, <p>, <img>.
- **Attributes**: Provide additional details. For example, the src attribute in the <img> tag specifies the image source (path of the file, where you kept it).

Example:

<img src="image.jpg" alt="Description of image">

- src="image.jpg": Specifies the image source (if kept in same folder where html file is).
- alt="Description of image": Provides an alternative text description for the image.

```
<div class="box">
  <div class="img-box">
    <img src="images/bajaj.png" alt="">
  </div>
```

- src="images/bajaj.png": Specifies the image source (kept inside image folder).
- alt="Description of image": helps browser to read what is in image.

CHAPTER 4: UNDERSTANDING WEB ELEMENTS AND STRUCTURE

4.1 Types of HTML Elements

HTML elements are categorized as:

- **Structural Elements**: These help organize the content on a page (e.g., <header>, <footer>, <section>).
- **Content Elements**: Elements that contain content (e.g., <p>, <h1>, <ul>, <li>).
- **Interactive Elements**: Elements that create user interactivity (e.g., <form>, <button>, <input>).
- **Multimedia Elements**: Elements used to embed media (e.g., <img>, <audio>, <video>).

Example:

- **Structural**: <header>, <footer>, <section>.
- **Content**: <p>, <h1>, <ul>.
- **Interactive**: <form>, <button>.

- *Let's create a new webpage from start and add some new elements and tag in it.*

- *Let's create a new file with any name you want and put .html as extension.*

```
Line wrap ☐
<!DOCTYPE html>
<html lang="en">
<head>
    <!-- Head section: Contains meta-information about the document -->
    <meta charset="UTF-8">
    <meta name="viewport" content="width=device-width, initial-scale=1.0">
    <title>Simple HTML Structure</title>
</head>
<body>

    <!-- Header Section: This is typically where the page title, navigation, or introductory content goes -->
    <header>
        <h1>Welcome to My Simple Page</h1>
    </header>

    <!-- Main Section: This contains the primary content of the page -->
    <section>
        <h2>Image and Form Section</h2>

        <!-- Image Container: A div containing an image -->
        <div>
            <img src="#" alt="Placeholder Image"> <!-- no source path, no image on display -->
        </div>

        <!-- Form Container: A div that holds the form elements -->
        <div>
            <form action="#" method="POST">
                <!-- Form Input: A text field where a user can type their name -->
                <label for="name">Name:</label>
                <input type="text" id="name" name="name" required>

                <!-- Form Input: A text field where a user can type their email -->
                <label for="email">Email:</label>
                <input type="email" id="email" name="email" required>

                <!-- Submit Button: A button to submit the form -->
                <button type="submit">Submit</button>
            </form>
        </div>
    </section>

    <!-- Footer Section: This contains the footer content of the page -->
    <footer>
        <p>&copy; 2025 My Simple Page</p>
    </footer>

</body>
</html>
```

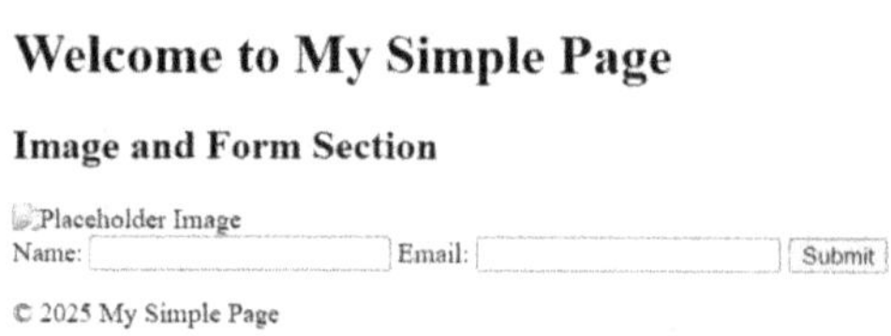

Explanation of the Tags:

- **<!DOCTYPE html>:** Specifies the document type and version of HTML being used (HTML5 here).
- **<html lang="en">:** The root element that wraps all the content in the HTML page. The lang attribute specifies the language as English.
- **<head>:** Contains metadata about the page, such as the character set, viewport settings, and the page title.
- **<meta charset="UTF-8">:** Specifies the character encoding for the page.
- **<meta name="viewport" content="width=device-width, initial-scale=1.0">:** Ensures the page is responsive on mobile devices.
- **<title>:** Sets the title of the web page that appears in the browser's tab.
- **<body>:** Contains the visible content of the page.
- **<header>:** Typically used to define the introductory content or navigation of the page.
- **<section>:** A block-level element that groups related content.
- **<div>:** A generic container for grouping elements, used here to wrap images and forms.
- **<img>:** Displays an image on the page. The src attribute defines the image source URL, and the alt attribute provides alternative text for accessibility.
- **<form>:** Represents a form for user input. The action attribute specifies where to send the form data, and method="POST" determines how the data is sent.
- **<input>:** Defines a field for user input (text and email fields here).

- **<label>:** Specifies labels for form controls.
- **<button>:** A clickable button used to submit the form.
- **<footer>:** Contains footer content, typically for copyright or contact information.

-

4.2 STYLING YOUR WEBPAGE: INTRODUCTION TO CSS

CSS is the language used for styling HTML elements. You can control properties like color, font size, margins, and layout.

Basic CSS Syntax:

```
body {
  background-color: lightblue;
  font-family: Arial, sans-serif;
}

h1 {
  color: darkblue;
  text-align: center;
}
```

This CSS code does two things:

1. Changes the background color of the body to light blue.
2. Centers the text inside the <h1> tag and changes its color to dark blue.

Line wrap

```
<!DOCTYPE html>
<html>
  <head>
    <title>My First Webpage</title>
  </head>
  <style>
  body {
  background-color: lightblue;
  font-family: Arial, sans-serif;
}

h1 {
  color: darkblue;
  text-align: center;
}

  </style>
  <body>
    <h1>Hello, World!</h1>
    <p>Welcome to my first webpage!</p>
    <a href="https://www.example.com">Click Here</a>
  </body>
</html>
```

*Here what we do is known as **Inline CSS**, where we do style or write css syntax in html file via using <style> tag. <style> has both opening and closing tag. Second method is writing code in separate css file having .css extension in end and link it with your html file. Don't worry we see this in another section.*

CHAPTER 5: STYLING YOUR WEBPAGE WITH CSS

5.1 Introduction to CSS

CSS (Cascading Style Sheets) is a language used to style the appearance of HTML elements. While HTML gives the webpage structure, CSS controls how it looks. The separation of structure (HTML) and style (CSS) allows for more flexibility and easier maintenance.

CSS is essential for:

- Changing colors, fonts, and text styles.
- Adjusting page layout and positioning.
- Adding animations or transitions.

5.2 How CSS Works: Selectors, Properties, and Values

In CSS, the **selector** targets an HTML element, while the **property** defines what aspect of the element you want to change, and the **value** specifies the new value.

/ this syntax is used to comment in css */ , and its different from what we do in HTML file, remember that always.*

Basic Syntax:

Selector {

```
  property: value;
}
```

Example:

```
h1 {
  color: blue; /* color is a property and blue is its value */
  text-align: center; /* same here, text-align is property and center is value */
}
```

CSS has many properties you can learn more about these properties via simple google search.

EXPLANATION:

- **h1**: This is the **selector**, targeting all <h1> elements.
- **color: blue**: The **property** is color, and the **value** is blue.
- **text-align: center**: The **property** is text-align, and the **value** is center.

- This rule changes the color of all <h1> elements to blue and centers the text.

Line wrap

```
<!DOCTYPE html>
<html>
  <head>
    <title>My First Webpage</title>
  </head>
  <style>
  body {
  background-color: lightblue;
  font-family: Arial, sans-serif;
    }

h1 {
  color: blue;
  text-align: center;
  }


  </style>
  <body>
    <h1>Hello, World!</h1>
    <p>Welcome to my first webpage!</p>
    <a href="https://www.example.com">Click Here</a>
  </body>
</html>
```

5.3 ADDING COLORS AND BACKGROUNDS

CSS allows you to easily apply colors to the text, background, and other elements.

Syntax for Colouring:

```
selector {
  color: color_value;    /* Text color, can be simple as name or in hexadecimal value */
  background-color: color_value;  /* Background color, */
}
```

Example:

```
body {
  background-color: lightgray;
  color: darkblue;
}
```

- **background-color: lightgray**: Sets the webpage

background color to light gray.

- **color: darkblue**: Changes the text color to dark blue.

You can use various color values such as:

- **Named colors**: red, blue, green, black
- **Hex values**: #ff5733 (for a specific shade), #fff (for white)
- **RGB values**: rgb(255, 87, 51)

```
<!DOCTYPE html>
<html>
  <head>
    <title>My First Webpage</title>
  </head>
  <style>
body {
  background-color: black;
  color: #fff;
}


h1 {
  color: blue;
  text-align: center;
  }


  </style>
  <body>
    <h1>Hello, World!</h1>
    <p>Welcome to my first webpage!</p>
    <a href="https://www.example.com">Click Here</a>
  </body>
</html>
```

5.4 WORKING WITH FONTS IN CSS

Fonts control the text appearance. In CSS, you can modify the font type, size, style, and weight.

Example of Font Styling:

```
h1 {
  font-family: 'Arial', sans-serif;
  font-size: 36px;
  font-weight: bold;
}
```

- **font-family**: Specifies the font. You can use system fonts like Arial or web fonts like Google Fonts.
- **font-size**: Sets the size of the font.
- **font-weight**: Makes the text bold or normal.

5.5 SPACING AND LAYOUT

CSS lets you control spacing between elements with properties like **margin** and **padding**.

- **Margin**: Space outside the element, pushing other elements away.
- **Padding**: Space inside the element, between the content and the border.

Example:

```
div {
  margin: 20px;
  padding: 10px;
  border: 1px solid black;
}
```

- **margin: 20px**: Creates a 20px space around the entire div.
- **padding: 10px**: Adds 10px space between the content inside the div and its border.

5.6 CSS Box Model

The **Box Model** is fundamental to understanding how elements are sized and spaced on a webpage. Every HTML element is treated as a box that consists of:

1. **Content**: The actual content, like text or images.
2. **Padding**: Space around the content inside the box.
3. **Border**: A line that surrounds the padding and content.
4. **Margin**: Space outside the border.

Example of Box Model:

This creates a div that is 300px wide, with 10px padding, 1px black border, and 20px margin.

```
div {
  width: 300px;
  padding: 10px;
  border: 1px solid black;
  margin: 20px;
}
```

CHAPTER 6: ADDING MEDIA TO YOUR WEBSITE

6.1 Adding Images

Images can be embedded in a webpage using the <img> tag. The **src** attribute defines the image source, and **alt** provides alternative text for screen readers.

Syntax:

<img src="image.jpg" alt="Description of image">

Example:

<img src="https://example.com/images/photo.jpg" alt="A beautiful landscape">

This code displays the image located at photo.jpg and adds a description for accessibility.

6.2 IMAGE FORMATS

The most common image formats are:

- **JPEG**: Best for photographs (lossy compression).
- **PNG**: Best for images with transparent backgrounds.
- **GIF**: Best for simple graphics or animated images.

You can use different formats to optimize website performance and load times.

6.3 ADDING VIDEOS

Adding videos enhances user experience, especially for educational or entertainment websites. You can embed a video directly using the <video> tag.

Syntax:

```
<video controls>
  <source src="video.mp4" type="video/mp4">
  Your browser does not support the video tag.
</video>
```

- **controls**: Provides video controls like play, pause, volume, etc.
- **<source>**: Specifies the video file and its format.

6.4 WORKING WITH AUDIO

Just like videos, you can add audio files to your website using the <audio> tag.

Syntax:

```
<audio controls>
  <source src="audio.mp3" type="audio/mp3">
  Your browser does not support the audio tag.
</audio>
```

- **controls**: Allows users to play, pause, and control the volume of the audio.

CHAPTER 7: BUILDING AND STRUCTURING YOUR WEBPAGE

7.1 Basic Webpage Structure

A basic webpage structure consists of the following key elements:

1. **Header**: Contains the website title, logo, and navigation links.
2. **Main Content**: The core content of the page, such as text, images, or forms.
3. **Footer**: Contains copyright, privacy policy links, or contact information.

```
<!DOCTYPE html>
<html lang="en">
  <head>
    <meta charset="UTF-8">
    <meta name="viewport" content="width=device-width, initial-scale=1.0">
    <title>My Webpage</title>
  </head>
  <body>
    <header>
      <h1>Welcome to My Website</h1>
      <nav>
        <a href="#home">Home</a>
        <a href="#about">About</a>
```

```
      <a href="#contact">Contact</a>
    </nav>
  </header>

  <main>
    <section>
      <h2>About Us</h2>
      <p>This is the section where you describe your website or business.</p>
    </section>

    <section>
      <h2>Contact Us</h2>
      <p>Here is how users can get in touch with you.</p>
    </section>
  </main>

  <footer>
    <p>© 2025 My Webpage. All Rights Reserved.</p>
  </footer>
</body>
</html>
```

Example:

This code creates a simple webpage with a header, main content sections, and footer. The **<nav>** tag holds navigation links that allow users to move around the site.

7.2 CREATING A LAYOUT WITH CSS

To structure the layout of your webpage, you can use different CSS layout techniques like **Flexbox**, **Grid**, and **Positioning**.

Flexbox:

Flexbox makes it easier to align items in rows or columns. It can be used for both horizontal and vertical layouts.

Example:

```
.container {
  display: flex;
  justify-content: space-between;
}
```

- **display: flex**: Defines a flex container.
- **justify-content: space-between**: Distributes the items evenly across the available space.

HTML:

```
<div class="container">
  <div>Item 1</div>
  <div>Item 2</div>
  <div>Item 3</div>
</div>
```

This creates a row with evenly spaced items.

7.3 STYLING FORMS IN HTML

Forms are crucial for gathering user input, such as contact details or feedback. You can create forms using the <form> tag.

Example:

```
<form action="/submit" method="POST">
  <label for="name">Name:</label>
  <input type="text" id="name" name="name">

  <label for="email">Email:</label>
  <input type="email" id="email" name="email">

  <button type="submit">Submit</button>
</form>
```

Explanation :

- **action**: The URL where the form data is sent.
- **method**: Specifies how to send the form data (usually GET or POST).
- **<input>**: Collects user input, such as text or email.
- **<button>**: Triggers the form submission.

HTML TAGS REVISION WITH EXAMPLES

This list provides essential HTML tags and CSS properties along with examples of how to use them in real-world scenarios. Understanding these elements is key to creating well-structured and visually appealing websites. As you get more comfortable with HTML and CSS, you can explore more advanced topics such as CSS Grid, Flexbox, and complex animations.

1. <!DOCTYPE html>

Defines the document type and HTML version (HTML5 in this case).

Example:

```
<!DOCTYPE html>
<html lang="en">
  <head>
    <meta charset="UTF-8">
    <title>Example Page</title>
  </head>
  <body>
    <h1>Welcome to My Webpage</h1>
  </body>
</html>
```

---

2. <html>

Defines the root element of an HTML document.

Example:

```
<html>
  <head>
    <title>My Page</title>
  </head>
  <body>
    <h1>Welcome to my website!</h1>
  </body>
</html>
```

---

3. <head>

Contains metadata, links to stylesheets, and scripts.

Example:

```
<head>
  <meta charset="UTF-8">
  <title>My Webpage</title>
  <link rel="stylesheet" href="styles.css">
</head>
```

---

4. <body>

Contains the content of the webpage (what the user sees).

Example:

```
<body>
  <h1>Hello, World!</h1>
  <p>This is a simple webpage.</p>
</body>
```

---

5. <h1> to <h6>

Defines headings with six levels, <h1> being the largest and <h6> the smallest, with closing tags </h1>.

Example:

```
<h1>Main Heading</h1>
<h2>Subheading</h2>
<h3>Sub-Subheading</h3>
```

---

6. <p>

Defines a paragraph.

Example:

```
<p>This is a paragraph of text.</p>
```

---

7. <a>

Creates a hyperlink.

Example:

```
<a href="https://www.example.com">Visit Example</a>
```

---

8. <img>

Embeds an image.

Example:

```
<img src="image.jpg" alt="Description of Image">
```

---

9. <form>

Defines an HTML form and it fields for collecting user input.

Example:

```
<form action="/submit" method="POST">
  <input type="text" name="username" placeholder="Enter your
```

```
username">
  <button type="submit">Submit</button>
</form>
```

---

10. <input>

Defines an input field in a form.

Example:

```
<input type="email" name="email" placeholder="Enter your email">
```

CSS Properties with Examples

1. color

Sets the text color of an element.

Example:

```
h1 {
  color: blue;
}
```

---

2. font-family

Defines the font type for the text.

Example:

```
p {
  font-family: 'Arial', sans-serif;
}
```

---

3. font-size

Sets the size of the text.

Example:

```
h1 {
```

```
  font-size: 36px;
}
```

---

4. font-weight

Sets the weight (thickness) of the font.

Example:

```
h2 {
  font-weight: bold;
}
```

---

5. text-align

Aligns the text (left, center, right).

Example:

```
p {
  text-align: center;
}
```

---

6. line-height

Sets the space between lines of text.

Example:

```
p {
  line-height: 1.5;
}
```

---

7. background-color

Sets the background color of an element.

Example:

```
body {
  background-color: lightgray;
}
```

---

8. border

Defines a border around an element.

Example:

```
div {
  border: 2px solid black;
}
```

---

9. width

Sets the width of an element.

Example:

```
div {
  width: 500px;
}
```

10. height

Sets the height of an element.

Example:

```
div {
  height: 300px;
}
```

---

11. padding

Sets the space between the content and the border of an element.

Example:

```
div {
  padding: 20px;
}
```

---

12. margin

Sets the space around an element, outside its border.

Example:

```
div {
  margin: 10px;
}
```

---

13. display

Defines how an element is displayed (block, inline, flex, grid).

Example:

```
div {
  display: flex;
}
```

---

14. flex-direction

Specifies the direction of flex items (row, column).

Example:

```
.container {
  display: flex;
  flex-direction: row;
}
```

15. justify-content

Aligns flex items along the main axis (start, center, space-between).

Example:

```
.container {
  display: flex;
  justify-content: center;
}
```

16. align-items

Aligns flex items along the cross-axis (top, center, stretch).

Example:

```
.container {
  display: flex;
  align-items: center;
}
```

17. box-shadow

Applies a shadow effect to an element.

Example:

```
div {
  box-shadow: 10px 10px 15px rgba(0, 0, 0, 0.5);
}
```

18. border-radius

Rounds the corners of an element.

Example:

```
div {
  border-radius: 10px;
}
```

---

19. opacity

Sets the opacity of an element, making it transparent.

Example:

```
img {
  opacity: 0.5;
}
```

---

20. transition

Defines the transition effect when a property changes.

Example:

```
div {
  background-color: blue;
  transition: background-color 0.3s ease;
}
div:hover {
  background-color: red;
}
```

---

21. @keyframes

Defines the animation sequence.

Example:

```
@keyframes fadeIn {
  from {
    opacity: 0;
  }
  to {
    opacity: 1;
  }
}

div {
  animation: fadeIn 2s ease-in-out;
}
```

---

22. grid-template-columns

Defines the number and size of columns in a grid layout.

Example:

```
.container {
```

```
  display: grid;
  grid-template-columns: 1fr 1fr 1fr;
}
```

---

23. grid-gap

Defines the gap between grid items.

Example:

```
.container {
  display: grid;
  grid-gap: 20px;
}
```

---

24. list-style-type

Defines the type of list item marker (circle, square, decimal).

Example:

```
ul {
  list-style-type: square;
}
```

ADVANCED STYLING WITH CSS

Advanced CSS styling allows developers to create dynamic, responsive, and visually engaging websites. By mastering concepts like **Flexbox**, **CSS Grid**, **Animations**, **Transitions**, and **Responsive Design**, you can take your web designs to the next level. Below, we delve deeper into these advanced techniques with detailed explanations and examples.

---

1. CSS Flexbox

Flexbox is a one-dimensional layout model that provides a flexible way to align and distribute space among items within a container. It is highly useful for creating responsive layouts that adapt to different screen sizes.

How Flexbox Works

The key concept of Flexbox is the **flex container** and the **flex items**. The flex container defines the layout behavior, while the flex items are the children inside the container that will be arranged according to the flexbox properties.

- **display: flex** is used on the container to activate the flex model.
- **justify-content** controls the alignment of items along the horizontal axis (main axis).
- **align-items** controls the alignment along the vertical axis (cross-axis).

```
<!DOCTYPE html>
<html lang="en">
<head>
  <meta charset="UTF-8">
  <meta name="viewport" content="width=device-width, initial-scale=1.0">
  <title>Flexbox Example</title>
  <style>
    .container {
      display: flex;
      justify-content: space-between; /* Distributes space evenly between items */
      align-items: center; /* Centers items vertically */
      height: 100vh;
      background-color: lightgray;
    }

    .item {
      background-color: lightblue;
      padding: 20px;
      border-radius: 5px;
    }
  </style>
</head>
<body>
  <div class="container">
    <div class="item">Item 1</div>
    <div class="item">Item 2</div>
    <div class="item">Item 3</div>
  </div>
</body>
</html>
```

Example:

- **justify-content: space-between;** ensures the items are spaced evenly with the first and last items at the edges.
- **align-items: center;** vertically centers the items within the container.

---

2. CSS Grid

CSS Grid is a two-dimensional layout system, which means it allows you to design both columns and rows simultaneously. This flexibility makes it ideal for building complex web layouts.

How CSS Grid Works

CSS Grid uses a **grid container** and **grid items**. In the grid container, you define the number of columns and rows. You then place grid items within the grid to define how they should behave in each section.

- **display: grid** activates the grid model on the container.
- **grid-template-columns** defines the number of columns and their sizes.
- **grid-gap** or **gap** creates space between grid items.

Example:

```html
<!DOCTYPE html>
<html lang="en">
<head>
  <meta charset="UTF-8">
  <meta name="viewport" content="width=device-width, initial-scale=1.0">
  <title>CSS Grid Example</title>
  <style>
    .container {
      display: grid;
      grid-template-columns: repeat(3, 1fr); /* Create 3 equal columns */
      gap: 20px; /* Space between items */
    }

    .item {
      background-color: lightgreen;
      padding: 20px;
      border-radius: 5px;
    }
  </style>
</head>
<body>
  <div class="container">
    <div class="item">Item 1</div>
    <div class="item">Item 2</div>
    <div class="item">Item 3</div>
  </div>
</body>
</html>
```

- **grid-template-columns: repeat(3, 1fr);** defines three columns, each taking up one fraction of available space (equal width).
- **gap: 20px;** creates a 20px space between each grid item.

3. CSS Animations

CSS animations allow you to add motion and transitions to elements on a page. Using the @keyframes rule, you can define the starting and ending states of an animation and how it transitions between those states.

How CSS Animations Work

- **@keyframes** defines the steps in an animation.
- **animation** applies the animation to the element.

Example:

This text fades in!

```
<!DOCTYPE html>
<html lang="en">
<head>
  <meta charset="UTF-8">
  <meta name="viewport" content="width=device-width, initial-scale=1.0">
  <title>CSS Animation Example</title>
  <style>
    @keyframes fadeIn {
      from {
        opacity: 0;
      }
      to {
        opacity: 1;
      }
    }

    .animated {
      animation: fadeIn 2s ease-in-out;
    }
  </style>
</head>
<body>
  <div class="animated">This text fades in!</div>
</body>
</html>
```

- **@keyframes fadeIn** animates the element from opacity: 0 (invisible) to opacity: 1 (visible).
- **animation: fadeIn 2s ease-in-out;** applies the fadeIn animation, which lasts 2 seconds and uses an easing function for a smooth transition.

4. CSS Transitions

CSS transitions provide a way to smoothly transition between different states of an element when a property changes. Transitions allow elements to change gradually, rather than instantly.

How CSS Transitions Work

- **transition** defines the property to transition, the duration, and the timing function.

Example:

Before Hover

After Hover

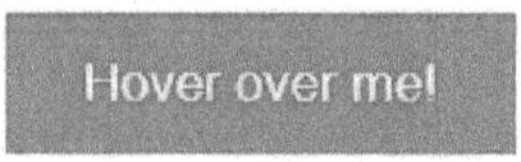

```
<!DOCTYPE html>
<html lang="en">
<head>
  <meta charset="UTF-8">
  <meta name="viewport" content="width=device-width, initial-scale=1.0">
  <title>CSS Transition Example</title>
  <style>
    button {
      background-color: blue;
      color: white;
      padding: 10px 20px;
      border: none;
      cursor: pointer;
      transition: background-color 0.3s ease;
    }

    button:hover {
      background-color: red;
    }
  </style>
</head>
<body>
  <button>Hover over me!</button>
</body>
</html>
```

- **transition: background-color 0.3s ease;** ensures that when the button is hovered over, the background color transitions from blue to red over 0.3 seconds, with an easing function for smoothness.

---

5. Responsive Design with Media Queries

Responsive design ensures that your website looks good and functions well on all devices, from smartphones to desktop computers. **Media queries** are used to apply styles based on different screen sizes and device characteristics.

How Media Queries Work

- **@media** defines the conditions under which certain styles should be applied (e.g., screen size or resolution).
- Media queries help you create breakpoints that adapt the layout and design of your site based on the device's width or height.

Example:

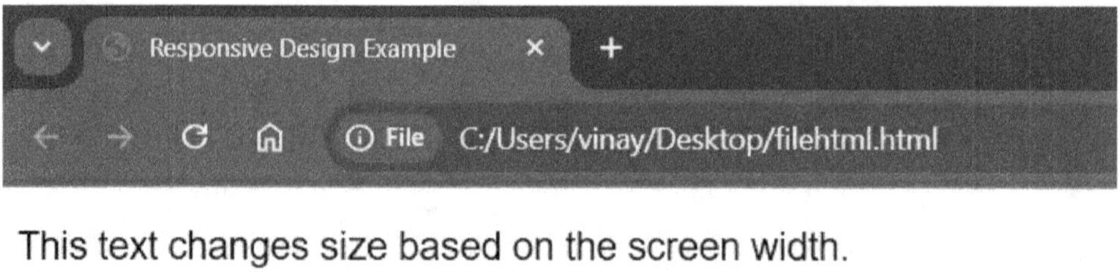

Line wrap

```
<!DOCTYPE html>
<html lang="en">
<head>
  <meta charset="UTF-8">
  <meta name="viewport" content="width=device-width, initial-scale=1.0">
  <title>Responsive Design Example</title>
  <style>
    body {
      font-family: Arial, sans-serif;
      font-size: 18px;
    }

    @media (max-width: 768px) {
      body {
        font-size: 16px; /* Smaller font size on smaller screens */
      }
    }

    @media (max-width: 480px) {
      body {
        font-size: 14px; /* Even smaller font size for very small screens */
      }
    }
  </style>
</head>
<body>
  <p>This text changes size based on the screen width.</p>
</body>
</html>
```

- **@media (max-width: 768px)** applies the style if the screen width is 768px or less (typically for tablets).
- **@media (max-width: 480px)** applies the style for very small screens (usually mobile phones).

Conclusion:

These advanced CSS techniques enable web developers to create modern, responsive, and visually appealing websites. By mastering **Flexbox** for layout management, **CSS Grid** for complex grids, **CSS Animations and Transitions** for dynamic effects, and **Media Queries** for responsive design, you can build user-friendly and interactive websites that work seamlessly across devices.

CHAPTER 8: ADDITIONAL LEARNING TOOLS

In this chapter, we provide additional resources and learning tools to help you solidify your understanding of web development concepts. This section includes a **Question & Answer series**, **Interview questions**, and a **Glossary** to ensure you're well-prepared for both practical work and job interviews. Let's dive deeper into these valuable learning tools.

8.1 QUESTION & ANSWER SERIES

This section is dedicated to answering the most common questions related to web design and development. It addresses frequently asked questions, troubleshooting tips, and provides some useful learning strategies to help accelerate your learning.

- **Frequently Asked Questions About Web Design**

Q1: What is the difference between HTML, CSS, and JavaScript?

- **HTML** (HyperText Markup Language) defines the structure of a web page. It's used to create the layout of your website and add content like headings, paragraphs, and images.
- **CSS** (Cascading Style Sheets) is used to style the web page. It controls the look and feel of the page, such as colors, fonts, layout, and spacing.
- **JavaScript** is a programming language that adds interactivity to your website. It is used to handle user actions like clicks, form submissions, and animations.

Q2: How do I make my website responsive?

- To make your website responsive, you need to use **CSS media queries**. Media queries adjust the styles of the page based on the size of the device's screen, ensuring it looks good on devices of all sizes (smartphones, tablets, and desktops).

Q3: Why do I need a CSS framework like Bootstrap?

- A CSS framework like **Bootstrap** provides pre-written CSS and JavaScript components that help you design websites quickly. It offers ready-made responsive grid systems, navigation bars, forms, and buttons, saving you time.

TROUBLESHOOTING COMMON ISSUES

Issue 1: My images are not loading on the web page.

- **Solution**: Check the image path in the src attribute of the <img> tag. Ensure that the file is in the correct directory relative to your HTML file.

Issue 2: My website looks different on different browsers.

- **Solution**: Browsers sometimes render elements differently. Use **CSS resets** (like normalize.css) to standardize the default styles across browsers. You can also use **vendor prefixes** to ensure compatibility with older browsers.

Issue 3: My website is not responsive.

- **Solution**: Make sure you've included the **meta tag** for the viewport in your HTML document:
- *<meta name="viewport" content="width=device-width, initial-scale=1.0">*

Additionally, use **media queries** to adjust your layout for different screen sizes.

- **Tips and Tricks to Speed Up Your Learning**
- **Practice regularly**: Web development is a skill that improves with consistent practice. Try building small projects daily or weekly.
- **Learn by doing**: The best way to learn is by actively

coding. Start with small tasks and gradually take on more complex challenges.

- **Use developer tools**: Every browser has built-in developer tools (F12 or right-click → Inspect). These tools allow you to inspect HTML/CSS, debug JavaScript, and test responsiveness.
- **Follow tutorials**: There are numerous free resources and tutorials available online, such as on platforms like **Learnincreation** or **MDN Web Docs or you can google search many more learning platform**.

8.2 INTERVIEW QUESTIONS

In this section, we will prepare you for job interviews in the web design and development field. We cover key interview questions, tips on how to prepare, and common mistakes to avoid during interviews.

- **Key Interview Questions for Web Design Jobs**

Q1: Can you explain the difference between class and id in CSS?

- **Answer**: In CSS, an **id** is used to select a single, unique element, while a **class** can be used to select multiple elements. The **id** should be used for one specific element on a page (e.g., the header), whereas the **class** can be applied to multiple elements (e.g., multiple buttons with the same style).
    - Example:
    - #header { /* Unique styling for header */}
    - .btn { /* Common styling for buttons */}

Q2: What is the CSS box model?

- **Answer**: The CSS **box model** defines the rectangular boxes generated for elements in the document tree. It consists of the following components:
    - **Content** (the actual content of the element),
    - **Padding** (space between content and border),
    - **Border** (surrounds padding),
    - **Margin** (space between the border and adjacent

elements).

Q3: How does the z-index property work in CSS?

- **Answer**: The **z-index** property controls the stacking order of elements that overlap. Elements with a higher z-index will appear above those with a lower z-index. This property works only on elements that have a **positioning context** (e.g., position: relative, absolute, or fixed).
    - Example:
    - .box1 { position: absolute; z-index: 2; }
    - .box2 { position: absolute; z-index: 1; }

• How to Prepare for a Web Development Interview

- **Know your basics**: Make sure you have a strong understanding of HTML, CSS, and JavaScript. Be ready to explain core concepts like the **DOM**, **responsive design**, and **browser compatibility**.
- **Prepare examples**: When asked technical questions, it's important to provide real-life examples of how you've used specific techniques in your projects.
- **Portfolio**: Bring a well-organized portfolio showcasing your best work. Include live links to your websites or repositories like GitHub.
- **Test your code**: Be prepared for live coding tests. Practice coding under time pressure to improve your problem-solving speed and accuracy.

• Common Mistakes to Avoid in Web Design Interviews

- **Not explaining your thought process**: When asked to solve a coding problem, always explain your thought process step-by-step.

- **Not preparing for non-technical questions**: Web development interviews also include behavioral questions. Be prepared to discuss your past projects, teamwork, and how you handle deadlines.
- **Overlooking responsive design**: With the increasing use of mobile devices, employers expect responsive, mobile-friendly websites. Always keep mobile-first design in mind.

8.3 GLOSSARY

In this section, we define essential web development terms that every beginner should understand. Familiarizing yourself with this glossary will ensure you speak the language of web development confidently.

- **Essential Web Development Terms You Should Know**

- **HTML (Hypertext Markup Language)**: The standard language for creating web pages. It defines the structure of the content on a webpage.
- **CSS (Cascading Style Sheets)**: A style sheet language used for describing the presentation of a document written in HTML or XML. It controls the layout, colors, fonts, and overall visual style of a webpage.
- **JavaScript**: A high-level programming language that adds interactivity to a webpage. It allows dynamic content updates, form validations, and user interaction.
- **Responsive Design**: An approach to web design that ensures websites work well on devices of all sizes by using flexible layouts, media queries, and scalable images.
- **DOM (Document Object Model)**: A programming interface for web documents. It represents the page so that programs can manipulate its structure, style, and content.

- **Understanding Key Terms in HTML, CSS, and JavaScript**

- **Element**: An HTML tag (e.g., <div>, <p>, <a>) that represents a piece of content on a webpage.
- **Selector**: In CSS, a selector targets an HTML element to apply styles. For example, .button targets all elements with the class button.
- **Function**: A block of reusable code in JavaScript that performs a specific task. For example, a function might calculate a value or update the webpage content.

  - **Quick Reference for Web Design Beginners**

- **HTML Tags**: HTML tags are enclosed in angle brackets and define the structure of a web page. Common tags include <html>, <head>, <body>, <p>, <a>, and <div>.
- **CSS Properties**: These are attributes used to style HTML elements, such as color, background, border, and font-size.
- **JavaScript Methods**: These are built-in functions in JavaScript, such as getElementById() to access HTML elements or addEventListener() to handle events.

Conclusion

This chapter, **Additional Learning Tools**, has equipped you with essential resources to further enhance your web development journey. By reviewing common questions, preparing for job interviews, and understanding the core terminology, you will be well on your way to becoming a skilled web developer.

CHAPTER 9: JAVASCRIPT FUNDAMENTALS (BONUS LESSON)

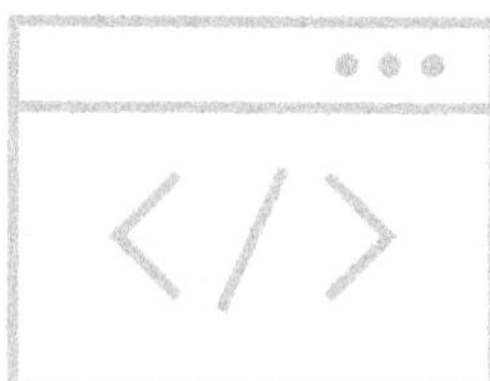

By understanding these JavaScript fundamentals, you've gained the skills to build dynamic, interactive websites. JavaScript provides the tools to manage user input, manipulate web page content, and make your pages more engaging and functional. With practice, you can master the core concepts and begin using JavaScript for more advanced web development tasks.

9.1 Introduction to JavaScript

JavaScript is one of the core web technologies alongside HTML and CSS, and it is used to create **dynamic** and **interactive** elements on web pages. While HTML provides the structure and CSS styles the content, JavaScript makes the page interactive by responding to user actions like clicks, keystrokes, and mouse movements.

For example, when you click a button and a popup appears, that action was likely made possible using JavaScript.

9.2 History of JavaScript

JavaScript was initially developed by **Brendan Eich** in 1995 while working for **Netscape Communications**. Originally named **Mocha**, it was later renamed **JavaScript**. It was initially used to create small interactive features on web pages, but as the language evolved, it became a powerful tool for building complex, full-featured websites.

Here's a brief overview of JavaScript's history:

- **1995**: JavaScript was first introduced under the name **Mocha**.
- **1997**: The first ECMAScript specification was published.
- **2005**: The rise of **AJAX** enabled JavaScript to create **dynamic** web pages.
- **2009**: **Node.js** allowed JavaScript to run on the server-side.
- **2015**: **ECMAScript 6 (ES6)** introduced major features like **arrow functions**, **classes**, and **let/const**.

9.3 JAVASCRIPT VERSIONS (ECMASCRIPT)

JavaScript's growth has been driven by updates and improvements, often formalized through **ECMAScript (ES)** versions. Here's a look at a few key versions:

1. **ECMAScript 3 (ES3)** - Released in **1999**: Added important features such as **regular expressions**.
2. **ECMAScript 5 (ES5)** - Released in **2009**: Introduced **strict mode**, which helps catch errors in JavaScript code.
3. **ECMAScript 6 (ES6)** - Released in **2015**: Introduced **let/const** (block-scoped variables), **arrow functions**, **promises**, **classes**, and **modules**.
4. **ECMAScript 7 (ES7)** - Released in **2016**: Introduced features like **Array.prototype.includes()**.
5. **ECMAScript 8 (ES8)** - Released in **2017**: Introduced **async/await** (for asynchronous programming), **Object.entries()**, and **Object.values()**.

9.4 JavaScript Fundamentals

In this section, we'll go into detail on the fundamental concepts of JavaScript. These concepts are the building blocks of the language and are essential for writing and understanding JavaScript code.

9.4.1 Data Types in JavaScript

In JavaScript, **data types** define the type of data that can be manipulated. There are two main types of data types:

1. **Primitive Data Types**: These are the most basic types in JavaScript.
   - String: Represents a sequence of characters.
   - let message = "Hello, World!";
   - console.log(message); // Output: Hello, World!
   - Number: Represents both integer and floating-point numbers.
   - let number = 25; // Integer
   - let price = 9.99; // Floating point number
   - console.log(number + price); // Output: 34.99
   - Boolean: Represents either true or false.
   - let isActive = true;
   - console.log(isActive); // Output: true
   - Null: Represents an intentional absence of any value.
   - let emptyValue = null;
   - console.log(emptyValue); // Output: null
   - Undefined: A variable that has been declared but not assigned any value.
   - let undefinedVar;
   - console.log(undefinedVar); // Output: undefined
2. **Non-Primitive Data Types**: These data types are more complex and include objects and arrays.
   - Object: A collection of key-value pairs.

- let person = {
- name: "John",
- age: 30,
- city: "New York"
- };
- console.log(person.name); // Output: John
- Array: A collection of ordered elements.
- let fruits = ["Apple", "Banana", "Cherry"];
- console.log(fruits[1]); // Output: Banana

9.4.2 OPERATORS IN JAVASCRIPT

Operators are used to perform operations on variables and values. JavaScript provides different types of operators:

1. **Arithmetic Operators**: Used for mathematical operations.
    - + (Addition)
    - - (Subtraction)
    - * (Multiplication)
    - / (Division)
    - % (Modulo)

Example:

```
let a = 10;
let b = 5;
console.log(a + b); // Output: 15 (Addition)
console.log(a - b); // Output: 5 (Subtraction)
console.log(a * b); // Output: 50 (Multiplication)
console.log(a / b); // Output: 2 (Division)
console.log(a % b); // Output: 0 (Modulo - remainder)
```

2. **Comparison Operators**: Used for comparing two values.
    - == (Equality)
    - === (Strict Equality)

- != (Inequality)
- > (Greater than)
- < (Less than)
- >= (Greater than or equal to)
- <= (Less than or equal to)

Example:

```
let x = 10;
let y = 20;
console.log(x == y); // Output: false (Equality)
console.log(x != y); // Output: true (Inequality)
```

3. **Logical Operators**: Used to combine multiple conditions.
    - && (AND)
    - || (OR)
    - ! (NOT)

Example:

```
let isAdult = true;
let isStudent = false;
console.log(isAdult && isStudent); // Output: false
console.log(isAdult || isStudent); // Output: true
```

9.4.3 FUNCTIONS IN JAVASCRIPT

A **function** is a block of code designed to perform a particular task. Functions can take inputs (called **parameters**) and return outputs (called **return values**).

1. **Function Declaration**: A function is declared using the function keyword followed by the function name and parameters.
2. function greet(name) {
3.   console.log("Hello, " + name);
4. }
5. greet("Alice"); // Output: Hello, Alice
6. **Function Expression**: A function can also be stored in a variable.
7. const add = function(a, b) {
8.   return a + b;
9. };
10. console.log(add(3, 5)); // Output: 8
11. **Arrow Function (ES6)**: Arrow functions provide a more concise way to write functions.
12. const multiply = (x, y) => x * y;
13. console.log(multiply(2, 3)); // Output: 6

Functions are reusable, making your code more modular and easier to maintain.

9.4.4 LOOPS IN JAVASCRIPT

Loops allow us to execute a block of code multiple times. JavaScript provides several types of loops:

1. **For Loop**: Used when you know how many times you want to loop.
2. *for (let i = 0; i < 5; i++) {*
3. *console.log(i); // Output: 0 1 2 3 4*
4. *}*
5. **While Loop**: Used when you want to loop as long as a condition is true.
6. *let i = 0;*
7. *while (i < 5) {*
8. *console.log(i); // Output: 0 1 2 3 4*
9. *i++;*
10. *}*
11. **Do-While Loop**: Similar to while, but ensures the code runs at least once.
12. *let i = 0;*
13. *do {*
14. *console.log(i); // Output: 0 1 2 3 4*
15. *i++;*

```
} while (i < 5);
```

9.4.5 ARRAYS IN JAVASCRIPT

An **array** is a collection of elements. Arrays in JavaScript can hold multiple values and are indexed from 0.

1. **Creating an Array**:
2. *let colors = ["red", "blue", "green"];*
3. *console.log(colors[1]); // Output: blue*
4. **Array Methods**:
    - push(): Adds an element to the end of the array.
    - colors.push("yellow");
    - console.log(colors); // Output: ["red", "blue", "green", "yellow"]
    - pop(): Removes the last element from the array.
    - colors.pop();
    - console.log(colors); // Output: ["red", "blue", "green"]
    - shift(): Removes the first element of the array.
    - colors.shift();
    - console.log(colors); // Output: ["blue", "green"]

9.4.6 OBJECTS IN JAVASCRIPT

An **object** is a collection of key-value pairs. It's a versatile data structure that allows you to group related data and functions together.

1. **Creating an Object**:
2. *let car = {*
3. *make: "Toyota",*
4. *model: "Corolla",*
5. *year: 2020*
6. *};*
7. *console.log(car.make); // Output: Toyota*
8. **Accessing Object Properties**: You can access object properties using **dot notation** or **bracket notation**:
9. *console.log(car["model"]); // Output: Corolla*

9.4.7 EVENT HANDLING IN JAVASCRIPT

Event handling is a key concept that allows you to make your website interactive. JavaScript can listen for events like clicks, key presses, and mouse movements.

1. **Event Listeners**: An event listener is a function that waits for a specific event to occur.
2. *let button = document.getElementById("myButton");*
3. *button.addEventListener("click", function() {*
4. *alert("Button clicked!");*
5. *});*
6. **Inline Event Handling**: You can also handle events directly in HTML using event attributes like onclick.
7. *<button onclick="alert('Button clicked!')">Click Me</button>*

9.4.8 DOM Manipulation

The **DOM (Document Object Model)** is the structure that represents your HTML document as an object, allowing you to manipulate the page's content using JavaScript.

1. **Selecting DOM Elements**:
    - **getElementById()**: Selects an element by its id.

- let header = document.getElementById("header");
- header.innerHTML = "Updated Header!";
- **querySelector()**: Selects the first matching element using a CSS selector.
- let firstButton = document.querySelector(".btn");

2. **Modifying DOM Content**: Use innerHTML or textContent to change the text or HTML inside an element.
3. *let message = document.getElementById("message");*
4. *message.innerHTML = "New message content!";*

Certainly! Let's dive deeper into **String Manipulation**, **Array Manipulation**, and **DOM Manipulation** in JavaScript. These are essential concepts for working with data and interacting with web pages and mastering them is key to becoming proficient in web development.

• String Manipulation in JavaScript

Strings are one of the most frequently used data types in JavaScript, and **manipulating strings** is a core aspect of the language. Here are some key methods and techniques to manipulate strings.

---

1. Concatenation

You can combine multiple strings into one using the + **operator** or the **concat()** method.

Using the + operator:

```
let greeting = "Hello, ";
let name = "John";
let message = greeting + name; // "Hello, John"
console.log(message);
```

Using the concat() method:

```
let message = greeting.concat(name); // "Hello, John"
console.log(message);
```

---

2. Finding the Length of a String

To get the number of characters in a string, use the length property.

```
let phrase = "Hello, world!";
console.log(phrase.length); // Output: 13
```

---

3. Accessing Characters in a String

To access individual characters, use the **charAt()** method or bracket notation.

Using charAt():

```
let word = "JavaScript";
console.log(word.charAt(0)); // Output: 'J'
```

Using bracket notation:

```
console.log(word[4]); // Output: 'S'
```

---

4. String Methods

JavaScript provides several built-in methods to manipulate and modify strings.

- **toUpperCase()**: Converts all characters in a string to uppercase.
- let text = "hello";
- console.log(text.toUpperCase()); // Output: "HELLO"
- **toLowerCase()**: Converts all characters in a string to lowercase.
- let text = "HELLO";
- console.log(text.toLowerCase()); // Output: "hello"
- **substring()**: Extracts a part of the string between two specified indices.
- let sentence = "I love JavaScript";
- console.log(sentence.substring(7, 17)); // Output: "JavaScript"
- **replace()**: Replaces part of the string with another string.
- let text = "I love JavaScript";
- let newText = text.replace("love", "enjoy");
- console.log(newText); // Output: "I enjoy JavaScript"
- **split()**: Splits a string into an array of substrings based on a delimiter.
- let sentence = "apple,banana,orange";
- let fruits = sentence.split(","); // ["apple", "banana", "orange"]
- console.log(fruits);

Array Manipulation in JavaScript

Arrays are an essential data structure in JavaScript that store multiple values. Here's how to manipulate arrays efficiently.

---

1. Creating and Initializing Arrays

You can create arrays using square brackets [].

let numbers = [1, 2, 3, 4, 5];

let fruits = ["apple", "banana", "orange"];

---

2. Accessing Array Elements

You can access array elements using an index (remember: indices in JavaScript are zero-based).

let numbers = [10, 20, 30];

console.log(numbers[0]); // Output: 10

---

3. Adding and Removing Elements

- **push()**: Adds an element to the end of an array.
- let numbers = [1, 2, 3];
- numbers.push(4); // [1, 2, 3, 4]
- **unshift()**: Adds an element to the beginning of an array.
- let numbers = [2, 3, 4];
- numbers.unshift(1); // [1, 2, 3, 4]
- **pop()**: Removes the last element from an array.
- let numbers = [1, 2, 3];
- numbers.pop(); // [1, 2]

- **shift()**: Removes the first element from an array.
- let numbers = [1, 2, 3];
- numbers.shift(); // [2, 3]

4. Iterating Over Arrays

- **forEach()**: Iterates over all elements of an array.
- *let fruits = ["apple", "banana", "orange"];*
- *fruits.forEach(function(fruit) {*
- *console.log(fruit); // Output: apple banana orange*
- *});*
- **map()**: Creates a new array by performing a function on each element.
- *let numbers = [1, 2, 3];*
- *let doubled = numbers.map(function(num) {*
- *return num * 2; // [2, 4, 6]*
- *});*
- *console.log(doubled);*

5. Array Manipulation Methods

- **filter()**: Filters out elements that don't satisfy a condition.
- let numbers = [1, 2, 3, 4, 5];
- let evenNumbers = numbers.filter(function(num) {
- return num % 2 === 0; // [2, 4]
- });
- console.log(evenNumbers);

- **reduce()**: Reduces an array to a single value by applying a function.
- let numbers = [1, 2, 3];
- let sum = numbers.reduce(function(accumulator, num)

{

- return accumulator + num; // 6
- }, 0);
- console.log(sum);

DOM Manipulation in JavaScript

The **Document Object Model (DOM)** represents the structure of a webpage, and JavaScript allows you to manipulate it to create interactive and dynamic web experiences.

---

1. Selecting DOM Elements

- **getElementById()**: Selects an element by its ID.
- let element = document.getElementById("myElement");
- console.log(element);
- **getElementsByClassName()**: Selects all elements with a specific class.
- let elements = document.getElementsByClassName("myClass");
- console.log(elements);
- **querySelector()**: Selects the first matching element based on a CSS selector.
- let firstButton = document.querySelector(".btn");
- **querySelectorAll()**: Selects all matching elements based on a CSS selector.
- let allButtons = document.querySelectorAll(".btn");

---

2. Modifying the DOM

- **Changing Text Content**: You can modify the text of an element using the textContent or innerHTML properties.

- let heading = document.getElementById("heading");
- heading.textContent = "New Heading Text";
- **Changing HTML Content**: Use innerHTML to modify the HTML inside an element.
- let container = document.getElementById("container");
- container.innerHTML = "<p>New paragraph content</ p>";
- **Changing Styles**: You can modify the styles of an element using the style property.
- let button = document.getElementById("myButton");
- button.style.backgroundColor = "blue";
- button.style.fontSize = "20px";

---

3. Creating New DOM Elements

You can dynamically create new elements and add them to the page using JavaScript.

- **Creating a New Element**:
- let newDiv = document.createElement("div");
- newDiv.textContent = "This is a new div!";
- document.body.appendChild(newDiv);

---

4. Event Handling and DOM Manipulation

Events allow interaction with the DOM by responding to user actions (like clicks, key presses, etc.).

- **Adding an Event Listener**:
- let button = document.getElementById("myButton");
- button.addEventListener("click", function() {
- alert("Button was clicked!");

```
• });
```

CONCLUSION

Mastering **string manipulation**, **array manipulation**, and **DOM manipulation** is essential for JavaScript developers. These techniques allow you to handle, manipulate, and interact with data and web page elements efficiently. As you continue practicing and exploring these features, you'll gain a deeper understanding of how to build dynamic, responsive websites.

JAVASCRIPT DATA STRUCTURES - DETAILED EXPLANATION

Data structures are crucial to organizing and managing data in a way that is efficient, easy to understand, and effective for various tasks. In JavaScript, we primarily work with **Arrays**, **Objects**, **Sets**, and **Maps**. Each of these data structures serves different purposes and can be used depending on the task at hand.

---

1. Arrays in JavaScript

What is an Array?

An **array** is an ordered collection of items. Arrays can store data of any type, such as strings, numbers, or even other arrays or objects. Arrays in JavaScript are zero-indexed, meaning the first element has an index of 0.

Creating an Array

You can create arrays in JavaScript in two ways:

- **Using array literals**: This is the most common way to create an array.
- let fruits = ["apple", "banana", "cherry"];
- **Using the new Array() constructor**:

- let fruits = new Array("apple", "banana", "cherry");

Accessing Elements

Array elements are accessed by their index. Since JavaScript arrays are zero-indexed, the first element is accessed with index 0.

let fruits = ["apple", "banana", "cherry"];

console.log(fruits[0]); // Output: "apple"

Modifying Elements

You can modify array elements by directly assigning a new value to an index.

let fruits = ["apple", "banana", "cherry"];

fruits[1] = "grape"; // Changing "banana" to "grape"

console.log(fruits); // Output: ["apple", "grape", "cherry"]

Common Array Methods

- **push()**: Adds an item to the end of the array.
- let fruits = ["apple", "banana"];
- fruits.push("cherry");
- console.log(fruits); // Output: ["apple", "banana", "cherry"]
- **pop()**: Removes the last item from the array.
- let fruits = ["apple", "banana", "cherry"];
- fruits.pop();
- console.log(fruits); // Output: ["apple", "banana"]
- **shift()**: Removes the first item from the array.
- let fruits = ["apple", "banana", "cherry"];
- fruits.shift();
- console.log(fruits); // Output: ["banana", "cherry"]

- **unshift()**: Adds an item to the beginning of the array.
- let fruits = ["banana", "cherry"];
- fruits.unshift("apple");
- console.log(fruits); // Output: ["apple", "banana", "cherry"]

Iterating Over an Array

You can use loops like for or forEach() to iterate through an array:

```
let fruits = ["apple", "banana", "cherry"];
fruits.forEach(function(fruit) {
  console.log(fruit); // Output: "apple", "banana", "cherry"
});
```

---

2. Objects in JavaScript

What is an Object?

An **object** is a collection of key-value pairs, where each key is a **property** and each value can be any valid data type (string, number, array, function, etc.). Objects are often used to represent real-world entities with properties and behaviors.

Creating an Object

You can create objects in JavaScript using **object literals**.

```
let person = {
  name: "John",
  age: 30,
  job: "Developer"
};
```

Accessing Object Properties

You can access the properties of an object using **dot notation** or **bracket notation**:

```
console.log(person.name); // Output: "John"
console.log(person["age"]); // Output: 30
```

Modifying Object Properties

You can change or add properties to an object as follows:

```
person.age = 31; // Updating a property
person.city = "New York"; // Adding a new property
console.log(person); // Output: { name: "John", age: 31, job: "Developer", city: "New York" }
```

Object Methods

Objects can also have methods (functions as object properties). Methods are used to perform actions or behaviors associated with the object.

```
let person = {
  name: "Alice",
  greet: function() {
    console.log("Hello, " + this.name);
  }
};
person.greet(); // Output: "Hello, Alice"
```

Example: Creating and Modifying an Object

```
let car = {
  make: "Toyota",
  model: "Camry",
  year: 2020,
  drive: function() {
```

```
    console.log("The car is driving");
  }
};

car.year = 2021; // Updating the year
car.color = "Red"; // Adding a new property
car.drive(); // Output: "The car is driving"
```

3. Sets in JavaScript

What is a Set?

A **Set** is a collection of values where each value must be unique. Unlike arrays, sets cannot contain duplicates. Sets are useful when you need to store a collection of unique values and when order matters.

Creating a Set

```
let numbers = new Set([1, 2, 3, 4, 5, 1]);
console.log(numbers); // Output: Set { 1, 2, 3, 4, 5 }
```

Adding and Removing Items

- **add()**: Adds a new element to the set. If the element already exists, it won't be added.
- numbers.add(6);
- console.log(numbers); // Output: Set { 1, 2, 3, 4, 5, 6 }
- **delete()**: Removes an element from the set.
- numbers.delete(3);
- console.log(numbers); // Output: Set { 1, 2, 4, 5, 6 }
- **clear()**: Removes all elements from the set.
- numbers.clear();

- console.log(numbers); // Output: Set {}

Checking for Existence

You can check if an item exists in the set using the **has()** method:

console.log(numbers.has(5)); // Output: true

console.log(numbers.has(3)); // Output: false

---

4. Maps in JavaScript

What is a Map?

A **Map** is a collection of key-value pairs, where both the keys and values can be any data type. Unlike objects, maps preserve the order of the inserted items and allow keys of any type (not just strings).

Creating a Map

let studentMap = new Map();

studentMap.set("name", "Alice");

studentMap.set("age", 25);

console.log(studentMap); // Output: Map { "name" => "Alice", "age" => 25 }

Accessing Map Values

You can access map values by using the **get()** method:

console.log(studentMap.get("name")); // Output: Alice

console.log(studentMap.get("age")); // Output: 25

Checking for Keys

To check if a key exists in the map, use the **has()** method:

console.log(studentMap.has("name")); // Output: true

console.log(studentMap.has("address")); // Output: false

Removing Items and Iterating Over Maps

- **delete()**: Removes an entry by its key.
- studentMap.delete("age");
- console.log(studentMap); // Output: Map { "name" => "Alice" }
- **forEach()**: You can use this method to iterate over a map.
- studentMap.forEach((value, key) => {
- console.log(key + ": " + value);
- });
- // Output: name: Alice

Summary of JavaScript Data Structures

- **Arrays**: Useful for ordered collections and lists. Arrays are index-based and provide many built-in methods like push(), pop(), shift(), and unshift().
- **Objects**: Used for storing key-value pairs where the key can be any string or symbol and the value can be any type of data.
- **Sets**: Collections of unique values. No duplicates allowed, making it ideal for tasks like removing duplicates from arrays.

- **Maps**: Key-value pairs, similar to objects, but with more flexibility in terms of data types for both keys and values.

By understanding and properly using these data structures, you can write more efficient and maintainable JavaScript code. Choose the right data structure based on your needs—whether you need to handle ordered lists, unique values, or complex key-value pairs—and your code will be optimized for the task at hand.

· JavaScript Question Answer Series

Here's a list of basic level **Question and Answer** related to **JavaScript** based on the concepts we discussed earlier.

1. What is JavaScript?

Ans: JavaScript is a versatile programming language that allows developers to create dynamic and interactive content for web pages. It enables web pages to respond to user actions, such as clicks, typing, or page navigation. JavaScript is primarily used to manipulate the DOM, handle events, and interact with web APIs.

---

2. What are the different data types in JavaScript?

Ans: JavaScript has seven fundamental data types:

1. **String**: Represents textual data, like "hello world".
2. **Number**: Represents numeric values, like 5, 10.5, or -3.
3. **Boolean**: Represents logical values, either true or false.
4. **Object**: A collection of key-value pairs used to store more complex data.
5. **Array**: A special type of object used to store ordered collections of data.
6. **Undefined**: Represents a variable that has been declared but not assigned a value.
7. **Null**: Represents an intentional absence of any object value.

---

3. How do you declare a variable in JavaScript?
Ans : In JavaScript, variables are declared using three keywords: var, let, and const.

- var: Used to declare variables in older JavaScript versions. It's function-scoped.
- let: Used to declare block-scoped variables.

- const: Used to declare constants, which cannot be reassigned.

Example:

```
let x = 10;

const name = "Alice";
```

4. What is an array in JavaScript and how do you create one?
Ans : An array is a special type of object used to store ordered collections of data. Arrays can hold multiple values in a single variable, and these values can be accessed using an index (starting from 0).

Example:

```
let fruits = ["apple", "banana", "cherry"];

console.log(fruits[0]); // Output: apple
```

---

5. What is an object in JavaScript?

Ans: An object is a collection of key-value pairs. In JavaScript, objects are used to store related data and functionality, such as properties and methods. An object can represent real-world entities.

Example:

```
let person = {

  name: "John", age: 30,

  greet: function() {

    console.log("Hello, " + this.name);

  }};
```

---

6. What are functions in JavaScript?

Ans: A function is a block of reusable code designed to perform a particular task. Functions allow you to avoid repetitive code and make your code more organized and maintainable.

Example:

```
function greet(name) {
  return "Hello " + name;
}
console.log(greet("Alice")); // Output: Hello Alice
```

---

7. How do JavaScript loops work?

Ans: Loops are used to execute a block of code multiple times. The most commonly used loops in JavaScript are for, while, and do-while loops.

Example of a for loop:

```
for (let i = 0; i < 5; i++) {
  console.log(i); // Output: 0, 1, 2, 3, 4
}
```

---

8. What is the purpose of if and else statements in JavaScript?

Ans : The if statement is used to execute a block of code only if a specified condition is true. If the condition is false, the else block can execute a different set of code.

Example:

```
let age = 18;
if (age >= 18) {
  console.log("You are an adult");
} else {
  console.log("You are a minor");
}
```

---

9. What is DOM manipulation?

Ans : The DOM (Document Object Model) represents the structure of a webpage. It allows JavaScript to interact with and manipulate the HTML and CSS of the page dynamically. Using JavaScript, you can modify elements, change styles, and add event listeners.

Example of changing text content:

```
document.getElementById("message").innerText = "Hello, JavaScript!";
```

---

10. What is an Event & How do you handle events in JavaScript?

Ans: An event is an occurrence that can be detected by JavaScript, such as a button click, mouse movement, or a key press. You can handle events by attaching event listeners to elements.

Example:

```
document.getElementById("btn").addEventListener("click", function() {
  alert("Button was clicked!");
});
```

---

11. What is a forEach() loop?

Ans: The forEach() method is an array method used to execute a provided function once for each element in an array. It does not return anything and is often used when you want to perform an action on each element of the array.

Example:

```
let numbers = [1, 2, 3];
numbers.forEach(function(num) {
  console.log(num * 2); // Output: 2, 4, 6
});
```

12. What is the difference between == and === operator in JavaScript?

Ans: The == operator checks for equality of values with type coercion, while the === operator checks for equality of both value and type, without type conversion.

Example:

```
console.log(5 == "5");  // true (because of type coercion)
console.log(5 === "5"); // false (because of type difference)
```

13. What is the this keyword in JavaScript?

Ans: The this keyword refers to the current object or context in which a function is called. It can behave differently depending on how and where the function is invoked.

Example:

```
let person = {
  name: "Alice",
  greet: function() {
    console.log("Hello " + this.name);
  }
};
person.greet();  // Output: Hello Alice
```

14. What is a null value in JavaScript?

Ans: null is a special value in JavaScript that represents the intentional absence of any object value. It is often used to signify that a variable has been explicitly set to no value.

Example:

```
let person = null; // person has no value
```

---

15. What is undefined in JavaScript?

Ans: undefined is a primitive value automatically assigned to variables that have been declared but not yet assigned a value. It also appears when a function doesn't explicitly return a value.

Example:

```
let x;

console.log(x); // Output: undefined
```

---

16. How do you define a function in JavaScript?

Ans: A function is defined using the function keyword followed by the function name, parentheses, and curly braces that contain the function's code.

Example:

```
function greet() {
  console.log("Hello, World!");
}
greet(); // Output: Hello, World!
```

These basic questions and answers will help you to clarify fundamental concepts of JavaScript and serve as a good starting point for you to strengthen their understanding of the language.

Here are 15 additional basic-level **JavaScript Question and Answer** that will help expand your understanding of JavaScript fundamentals:

Ques: What is an object in JavaScript, and how do you create one?
Ans: An object in JavaScript is a collection of key-value pairs where each key (also called a property) is a string, and each value can be

any data type. Objects can be used to represent real-world entities.

Example:

```
let car = {
  brand: "Toyota",
  model: "Corolla",
  year: 2020
};
```

Ques: What is the difference between let and const?
Ans : Both let and const are used to declare variables, but:

- let: Allows you to reassign the value of a variable.
- const: Creates a constant variable whose value cannot be changed after it is assigned.

Example:

```
let a = 5;
a = 10; // valid
const b = 20;
b = 30; // Error: Assignment to constant variable
```

Ques: What is the break statement, and how is it used in JavaScript?
Ans: The break statement is used to terminate a loop or switch statement prematurely, exiting it immediately.

Example:

```
for (let i = 0; i < 5; i++) {
  if (i === 3) {
    break; // Exits the loop when i equals 3
  }
```

```
  console.log(i);
}
// Output: 0, 1, 2
```

Ques: What does the continue statement do in JavaScript?
Ans : The continue statement is used to skip the current iteration of a loop and move to the next iteration.

Example:

```
for (let i = 0; i < 5; i++) {
  if (i === 3) {
    continue; // Skips the iteration when i equals 3
  }

console.log(i);
}
// Output: 0, 1, 2, 4
```

Ques: What is the typeof operator in JavaScript?
Ans : The typeof operator is used to check the data type of a variable or an expression.

Example:

```
let num = 5;
console.log(typeof num); // Output: number
let name = "Alice";
console.log(typeof name); // Output: string
```

Ques : What is an arrow function in JavaScript, and how is it different from a regular function?
Ans : Arrow functions are a shorter syntax for writing functions

in JavaScript. They also bind this lexically, meaning they don't create their own this value, unlike regular functions.

Example:

```
const greet = (name) => {
  console.log("Hello " + name);
};
greet("Bob"); // Output: Hello Bob
```

Ques: What are template literals, and how do they work?
Ans : Template literals are a feature in JavaScript that allow for multi-line strings and string interpolation. They are enclosed in backticks (` `) instead of quotes.

Example:

```
let name = "Alice";
let message = `Hello, ${name}! Welcome to JavaScript.`;
console.log(message); // Output: Hello, Alice! Welcome to JavaScript.
```

Ques: What is JSON in JavaScript, and how is it used?
Ans : JSON (JavaScript Object Notation) is a lightweight data interchange format that is easy for humans to read and write, and easy for machines to parse and generate. It is often used to send and receive data between a server and a client.

Example:

```
let jsonData = '{"name": "John", "age": 30}';
let obj = JSON.parse(jsonData); // Converts JSON string to JavaScript object
console.log(obj.name); // Output: John
```

Ques: What is the difference between null and undefined?
Ans :

- null represents the intentional absence of a value, usually assigned to a variable as a placeholder.
- undefined means a variable has been declared but has not been assigned a value yet.

Example:

```
let x = null;  // x has no value
let y;         // y is undefined
```

Ques: What is the window object in JavaScript?
Ans: The window object represents the browser's window and provides methods, properties, and events related to the browser's environment. It is the global object in the browser context.

Example:

```
window.alert("Hello, World!"); // Displays an alert box
```

Ques: What is a callback function, and how is it used in JavaScript?
Ans : A callback function is a function passed as an argument to another function and is executed after the completion of that function's task. It is widely used for handling asynchronous operations.

Example:

```
function greet(name, callback) {
  console.log("Hello " + name);
  callback();
}

function showMessage() {
  console.log("Welcome to JavaScript!");
}
```

```
greet("Alice", showMessage);
// Output: Hello Alice
// Output: Welcome to JavaScript!
```

Ques: How do you check if a variable is an array in JavaScript?
Ans: You can check if a variable is an array using the Array.isArray() method.

Example:

```
let arr = [1, 2, 3];
let notArray = { a: 1, b: 2 };
console.log(Array.isArray(arr));     // Output: true
console.log(Array.isArray(notArray)); // Output: false
```

Ques: What do setTimeout() and setInterval() do in JavaScript?
Ans :

- setTimeout() is used to execute a function after a specified delay (in milliseconds).
- setInterval() is used to repeatedly execute a function with a specified interval (in milliseconds).

Example:

```
setTimeout(() => {
  console.log("This will run after 3 seconds.");
}, 3000);
setInterval(() => {
  console.log("This will run every 2 seconds.");
}, 2000);
```

Ques: What is localStorage and how is it used in JavaScript?
Ans : localStorage is a Web API that allows you to store data in the browser without expiration. It is useful for saving user preferences or session data that persists even after the browser is closed. For example,

```
localStorage.setItem("name", "Alice");

let name = localStorage.getItem("name");

console.log(name); // Output: Alice
```

Ques: What is the try...catch statement used for in JavaScript?
Ans : The try...catch statement is used to handle errors in JavaScript code. It allows you to try a block of code and catch any errors that occur during execution. For example,

```
try {
  let result = 10 / 0;
  if (!isFinite(result)) {
    throw new Error("Division by zero");
  }
} catch (error) {
  console.log(error.message); // Output: Division by zero
}
```

Ques: How does the switch statement work in JavaScript?
Ans : A switch statement is used to evaluate multiple expressions based on a variable's value. It is an alternative to using multiple if...else statements.

Example:

```
let day = 2;

switch (day) {
```

```
  case 1:
    console.log("Monday");
    break;
  case 2:
    console.log("Tuesday");
    break;
  default:
    console.log("Invalid day");
}
// Output: Tuesday
```

These additional **JavaScript questions and answers** provide further insights into common JavaScript concepts and give clarity on key features and syntax. They will help anyone grasp fundamental knowledge of JavaScript more easily.

Now you made your First website with the help of HTML, CSS and JavaScript and now it's time to show your work to the fellow developer for shake of knowledge sharing or showing them what you made so far. We can use Github to keep our source code save and manage, to show them to other developer or keep a record of our work as a developer or project we made. So, let's learn bit about Github.

10. What is GitHub?

GitHub is a platform that provides hosting for software development and version control using **Git**. It allows developers to store their code in repositories, track changes, and collaborate with other developers. GitHub is widely used for both open-source and private projects.

Key Benefits of GitHub:

- **Version Control:** Track changes to your codebase over time, revert to previous versions, and compare code.
- **Collaboration:** Allows multiple developers to work on the same project without interfering with each other's work.
- **Backup:** Stores your code online, acting as a backup.
- **Public/Private Repositories:** You can choose to make your code public for others to contribute or keep it private.
- **Documentation:** You can add README.md files to explain your project, provide instructions, and share insights.

Now, let's go step-by-step on how to **push your website code into GitHub** after the completion of a project.

10.1 Step-by-Step Guide to Push Website Code to GitHub

Step 1: Create a GitHub Account

If you haven't already, create a **GitHub** account by visiting https:// github.com and signing up.

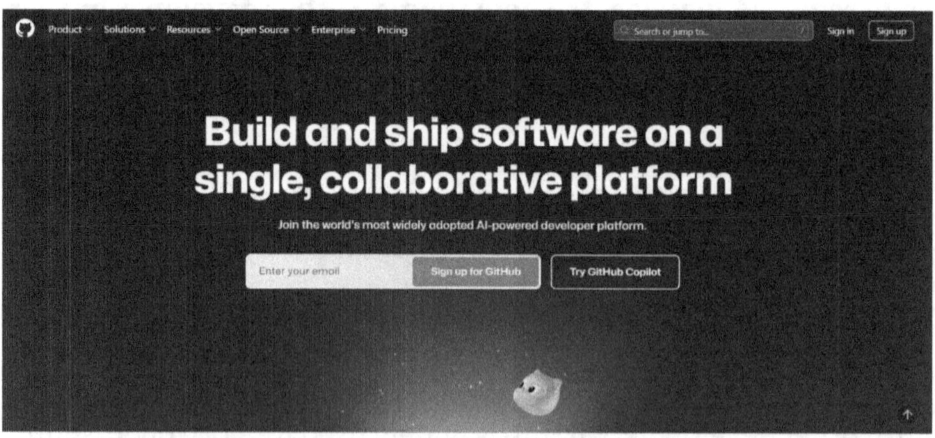

Step 2: Install Git Locally

Before you can use GitHub, you need to install **Git** on your local machine if you haven't already.

- **Windows**: Download Git from https://git-scm.com/downloads and install it.
- **Mac**: Use Homebrew or download directly from the Git website.
- **Linux**: Install via package manager. For example:
- sudo apt-get install git

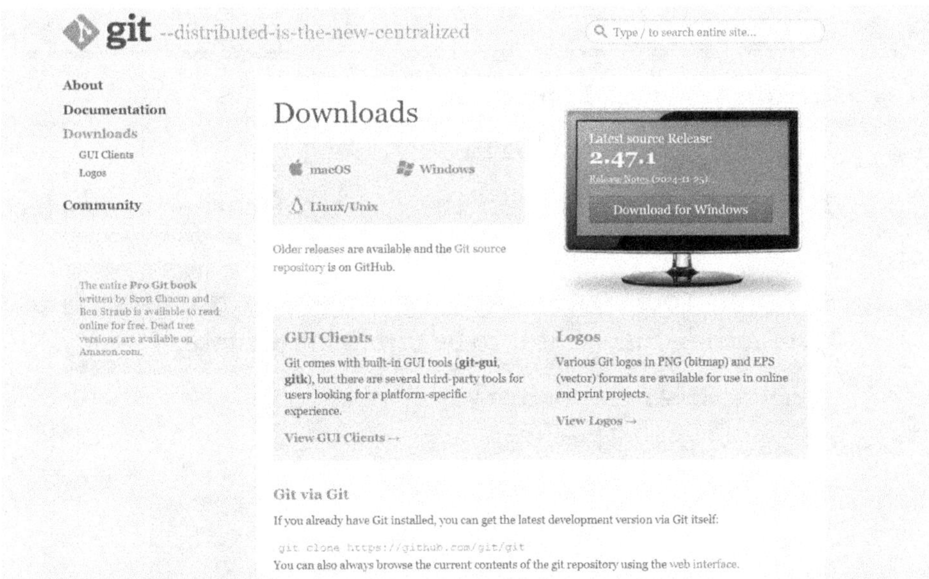

Step 3: Configure Git with Your GitHub Account

After installing Git, open your terminal (or Git Bash) and configure your username and email. This ensures your commits are associated with your GitHub account.

```
git config --global user.name "Your Name"

git config --global user.email "your.email@example.com"
```

Step 4: Initialize Git in Your Project Folder

1. Navigate to your project directory where your website files are located. For example:
2. cd path/to/your/website-folder
3. Run the following command to initialize a Git repository:
4. git init

This creates a .git folder in your project directory, signaling that the directory is now a Git repository.

Step 5: Create a GitHub Repository

1. Go to GitHub and log in.
2. Click the **"+" icon** on the top-right corner and select **"New repository"**.
3. Name your repository (e.g., my-website), and choose whether you want it to be **public** or **private**.
4. Click **Create repository**.

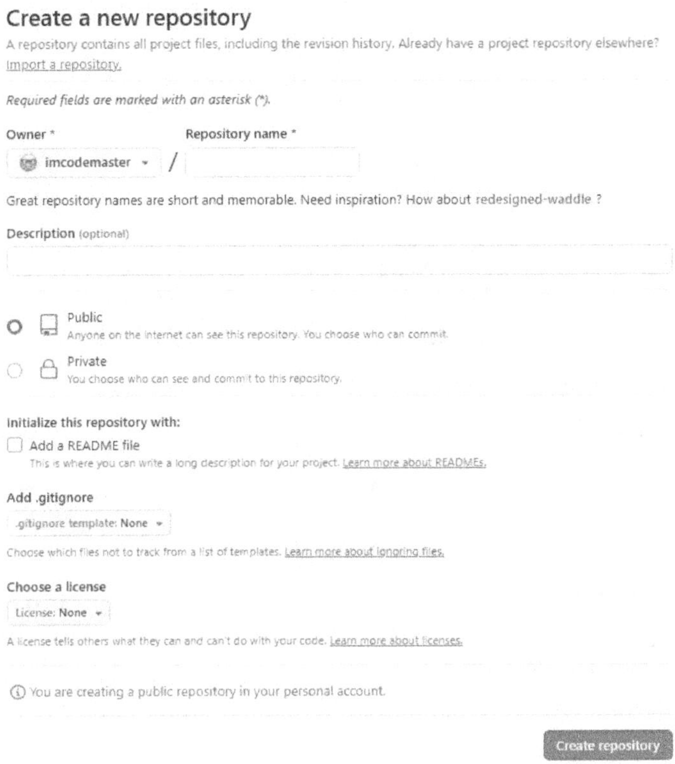

Step 6: Link Your Local Repository to GitHub

After creating your repository on GitHub, you will be provided with a **repository URL**. You will need this URL to push your local code to GitHub.

1. In your terminal, add the remote GitHub repository to your project:
2. git remote add origin https://github.com/username/my-website.git

Replace username with your GitHub username and my-website with the name of your repository.

Step 7: Add Files to the Git Repository

Now, you need to **stage** the files you want to commit.

1. To add all the files to the staging area:
2. git add .

This command stages all the files in your project folder, ready to be committed.

Step 8: Commit the Changes

Commit the staged files with a descriptive message. For example:

git commit -m "Initial commit of website project"

This creates a snapshot of the changes in your project and adds it to the Git history.

Step 9: Push Code to GitHub

Now, it's time to push your local repository to GitHub. Since you’ve already set up the remote origin, you can use the following command:

git push -u origin master

- -u sets the upstream branch to origin/master (so in the future, you can just use git push).
- origin refers to your GitHub repository.
- master is the branch you're pushing to (you can also use main instead of master if GitHub default branch is set to main).

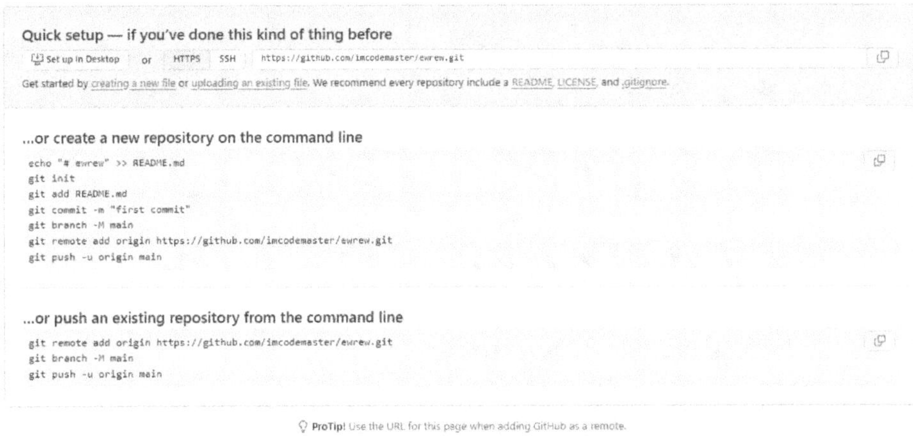

Step 10: Verify Code on GitHub

Once you have successfully pushed the code, visit your GitHub repository in your browser. You should see your website files listed there.

Step 11: Future Updates (Optional)

For future changes, after making modifications to your project, repeat these steps:

1. Add changes to the staging area:
2. git add .
3. Commit the changes:
4. git commit -m "Updated some content or fixed a bug"
5. Push the changes to GitHub:
6. git push

10.2 IMPORTANT GIT COMMANDS RECAP

1. **Initialize Git Repository**:
2. git init
3. **Add Changes** (Stage files):
4. git add .
5. **Commit Changes**:
6. git commit -m "Your commit message"
7. **Add Remote Repository**:
8. git remote add origin https://github.com/username/my-website.git
9. **Push Code to GitHub**:
10. git push -u origin master
11. **Pull Code from GitHub**:
12. git pull origin master
13. **Check Git Status**:
14. git status

Conclusion

By following these steps, you can easily push your completed website code into GitHub, which allows you to store, version, and share your code efficiently. GitHub makes collaboration much easier, and it serves as a reliable platform for both personal projects and teamwork. Understanding how to use Git and GitHub is essential for every developer as it streamlines project management and team collaboration.

Congratulations on Completing "Fun with Designing"!

You've come a long way in your journey to mastering **HTML**, **CSS**, and **JavaScript**, and now you have the foundation to start building impressive websites. With the knowledge and skills you've gained, you can confidently create static websites and bring your creative visions to life.

What's Next?

Now that you've learned the essentials of front-end web development, you might be wondering: "What's next for me?" The world of web development is vast, and there are many exciting paths to explore. If you're eager to take your skills to the next level and learn how to build **dynamic websites** and **web applications**, you're in the right place!

Learn Dynamic Website Creation with Python & Django

Ready to transition from static websites to fully interactive and dynamic web applications? Our next step is introducing you to **Python** and **Django**. This powerful combination allows you to build dynamic websites that interact with databases, handle user inputs, and more.

Why Python and Django?

- **Python** is one of the most popular programming languages today. It's simple to learn, yet incredibly powerful and versatile.

- **Django** is a high-level Python web framework that encourages rapid development and clean, pragmatic design. With Django, you can focus on building great websites without worrying about repetitive tasks like database handling, security, and scalability.

If you're interested in learning how to build dynamic websites, we invite you to check out our comprehensive guide, **"Web Development with Python & Django"**, available on **Amazon**. This book will walk you through building dynamic, data-driven websites, working with databases, handling user authentication, and deploying your web applications.

What You'll Learn in "Web Development with Python & Django"

- How to set up and configure a Django project
- How to create dynamic pages with data from databases
- User authentication, session management, and working with forms
- Deploying your application to a live server (e.g., Heroku, AWS)
- And much more!

Learn From Anywhere, Anytime!

The best part about our book is that you can learn from anywhere in the world, at your own pace. Whether you're a beginner or an intermediate developer, our book will guide you through each step with clear explanations, practical examples, and hands-on exercises.

Get Your Copy of "Web Development with Python & Django" Today!

Don't wait—your journey to mastering full-stack web development starts now! Head over to **Amazon.com** and get your copy of **"Web Development with Python & Django"**.

Get started now and take your web development skills to the next level!

- **Buy it now**: Find Vinay Bhatt books on Amazon.

Join the Web Development Community

Remember, learning to code is a journey, not a destination. Keep building, experimenting, and improving your skills. The web development community is vast and full of resources, and by continuing to learn and practice, you'll become a well-rounded developer in no time!

Thank you for reading "Fun with Designing", and we look forward to seeing you in the next stage of your web development journey with **Python and Django**. Happy coding!

JavaScript Glossary

A **Glossary** is a useful reference guide for beginners and experienced developers to familiarize themselves with common terms used in JavaScript programming. Below is a collection of essential JavaScript terms with brief definitions to help you better understand the language.

A

Array
A special variable used to store multiple values in a single variable. Arrays are ordered collections of data.
Example:

```
let fruits = ["apple", "banana", "cherry"];
```

Arrow Function
A shorthand way of writing function expressions in JavaScript. It uses the => syntax to define functions.
Example:

```
const add = (a, b) => a + b;
```

B

Boolean
A data type that has two possible values: true or false. Used for logical operations and condition checking.
Example:

```
let isActive = true;
```

Block
A group of statements or expressions enclosed in curly braces {}. Typically used in control structures like loops, if statements, and functions.
Example:

```
if (x > 10) {
  console.log("x is greater than 10");
```

```
}
```

C

Callback Function

A function passed as an argument to another function that gets executed later. Often used in asynchronous programming.
Example:

```
function fetchData(callback) {
  let data = "Hello World";
  callback(data);
}

fetchData(function(data) {
  console.log(data);
});
```

Class

A blueprint for creating objects in JavaScript. A class defines properties and methods that the objects created from it will have.
Example:

```
class Person {
  constructor(name, age) {
    this.name = name;
    this.age = age;
  }
}
```

Constructor

A special method inside a class used to initialize new objects created from the class.
Example:

```
class Car {
  constructor(make, model) {
    this.make = make;
    this.model = model;
  }
}
```

D

DOM (Document Object Model)
A programming interface for web documents. It represents the page so that programs can manipulate the structure, style, and content dynamically.
Example:

```
document.getElementById("myElement").innerHTML = "Hello World!";
```

Debugger
A tool that helps developers identify and fix bugs in their code by allowing them to step through it, watch variables, and inspect the execution flow.

E

Event
An action or occurrence recognized by the browser, such as a mouse click, key press, or page load. Events can trigger JavaScript functions.
Example:

```
document.getElementById("btn").addEventListener("click", function() {
  alert("Button clicked!");
});
```

Event Listener
A function that waits for specific events to occur on a webpage, such as clicks, hover, or keypress. It is used to execute code when the event is triggered.
Example:

```
document.querySelector("button").addEventListener("click",
function() {
  console.log("Button was clicked!");
});
```

F

Function
A block of code designed to perform a particular task. Functions are defined using the function keyword and can take arguments and return values.
Example:

```
function greet(name) {
  return "Hello " + name;
}
```

Function Expression
A function that is defined within an expression, often used as an anonymous function (without a name).
Example:

```
const greet = function(name) {
  return "Hello " + name;
};
```

G

Global Scope
A variable or function declared in the global scope can be accessed from anywhere in the JavaScript code, including functions and

blocks.
Example:

```
let globalVar = "I'm accessible everywhere";

function printGlobal() {
  console.log(globalVar);
}
```

H

Hoisting
The JavaScript mechanism where variables and functions are moved to the top of their scope before the code is executed.
Example:

```
console.log(x); // undefined
var x = 5;
```

I

If Statement
A conditional statement used to execute code based on whether a condition is true or false.
Example:

```
if (x > 10) {
  console.log("x is greater than 10");
}
```

Iterator
An object that defines a sequence and allows iterating over it. Commonly used with arrays or other iterable objects.
Example:

```
const arr = [1, 2, 3];
```

```
const iterator = arr[Symbol.iterator]();
console.log(iterator.next()); // { value: 1, done: false }
```

L

Literal
A notation for expressing fixed values directly in the code, such as strings, numbers, and arrays.
Example:

```
let x = 42; // numeric literal
let name = "John"; // string literal
```

Loop
A programming construct used to repeat a block of code a certain number of times or while a specific condition is true.
Example:

```
for (let i = 0; i < 5; i++) {
  console.log(i);
}
```

M

Method
A function that is associated with an object or class. Methods perform actions related to the object or class.
Example:

```
const person = {
  name: "Alice",
  greet: function() {
    console.log("Hello " + this.name);
  }
};
```

```
person.greet(); // Output: Hello Alice
```

O

Object
A collection of key-value pairs where each key is a string (property name) and each value can be any data type (primitive values, arrays, or other objects).
Example:

```
let car = {
  make: "Toyota",
  model: "Corolla",
  year: 2020
};
```

Operator
Symbols used to perform operations on values and variables. Examples include arithmetic operators (+, -, *, /) and logical operators (&&, ||, !).
Example:

```
let sum = 5 + 10; // + is an operator
```

P

Prototype
Every JavaScript object has a prototype property that allows it to inherit properties and methods from other objects.
Example:

```
let animal = {
  sound: "roar",
  speak: function() {
    console.log(this.sound);
  }
```

```
};
let tiger = Object.create(animal);
tiger.speak(); // Output: roar
```

R

Return
A keyword used to exit a function and optionally return a value.
Example:

```
function multiply(a, b) {
  return a * b;
}
```

S

String
A sequence of characters enclosed in quotes. Strings are commonly used to represent text.
Example:

```
let name = "John";
```

Switch Statement
A control structure used to compare a value against multiple cases and execute the code block corresponding to the matched case.
Example:

```
let day = 3;
switch(day) {
  case 1:
    console.log("Monday");
    break;
  case 2:
    console.log("Tuesday");
```

```
    break;
  case 3:
    console.log("Wednesday");
    break;
}
```

T

This
Refers to the current instance of an object in JavaScript. It is commonly used within methods to refer to the object itself.
Example:

```
let person = {
  name: "Alice",
  greet: function() {
    console.log("Hello, " + this.name);
  }
};
person.greet(); // Output: Hello, Alice
```

U

Undefined
A variable that has been declared but has not been assigned a value. Its default value is undefined.
Example:

```
let x;
console.log(x); // Output: undefined
```

V

Variable
A container used to store data. Variables can hold different types of values and are declared using var, let, or const.
Example:

```
let x = 5;
```

W

While Loop
A type of loop that executes as long as a given condition is true.
Example:

```
let i = 0;
while (i < 5) {
  console.log(i);
  i++;
}
```

This glossary serves as a quick reference for essential JavaScript terms. Understanding these concepts will provide a solid foundation for learning and mastering JavaScript.

Thanks for reading!

End Of Book

www.ingramcontent.com/pod-product-compliance
Lightning Source LLC
Chambersburg PA
CBHW062140160726
48282CB00027B/887
9789357806619